FROM
MOUNTAINTOP

FROM THE MOUNTAINTOP

An Archive History of Batley RLFC

John Roe
Terry Swift
Ken Pearson
Craig Lingard

Scratching Shed Publishing Ltd

Cover photograph: J B Goodall (Jack) and Harry Goodall.
Back cover: 'The Gallant Youths' 1897 –
winners of the inaugural Challenge Cup
(courtesy of *A 'Ton' Full of Memories*, Brian Cartwright, 1986)

A catalogue record for this book is available from the
British Library.

Typeset in Warnock Pro Semi Bold and Palatino
Printed and bound in the United Kingdom

TJ INTERNATIONAL
QUALITY BOOK MANUFACTURERS

Trecerus Industrial Estate, Padstow,
Cornwall PL28 8RW
www.tjinternational.ltd.uk

This book is dedicated
to each and every
Gallant Youth

Contents

Acknowledgements

A special thank you is owed to the National Lottery Heritage Fund which supported the project from which this book emerged.

A special thanks too to Scratching Shed Publishing from whom advice and guidance was readily forthcoming, and to the ever helpful staff at Batley Library for whom no request was ever too onerous.

Appreciation is also due to the British Newspaper archive and to the following publications from which various items have been extracted: *Athletic News, Batley News, Batley News and Birstall Advertiser, Batley Reporter, Birmingham Daily Post, Bolton Evening News, Bradford Daily Telegraph, Bradford Observer, Bradford Telegraph, Coventry Evening Telegraph, Daily Express, Dewsbury Reporter, Driffield Times, Dundee Courier and Argus, Eastern Morning News, Hartlepool Daily Mail, Huddersfield Daily Chronicle, Hull Daily Mail, The Independent, Lancashire Daily Post, Lancashire Evening Post, Leeds and*

Acknowledgements

Yorkshire Mercury, Leeds Intelligencer, Leeds Mercury, Leeds Times, Leigh Chronicle, Liverpool Daily Post, Liverpool Echo, Liverpool Mercury, London Daily News, London Evening Standard, Manchester Courier, Manchester Evening News, Midland Daily Telegraph, Millom Gazette, Otley and Ilkely Guardian, Portsmouth Evening News, Sheffield Daily Independent, Sheffield Daily Telegraph, Sheffield Star, Sheffield Star Green 'Un', Shipley Times and Express, South Wales Daily News, Sporting Life, Sports Special 'Green Un', Sportsman, The People, Todmorden Advertiser, Western Daily Press, Bristol, Western Mail. South Wales News, Wharfedale and Airedale Observer, York Herald, Yorkshire Evening Post, Yorkshire Herald, Yorkshire Post, Yorkshire Post and Leeds Intelligencer.

A *'Ton' Full of Memories* – Brian Cartwright 1986; *The Gallant Youths* – Charles F Shaw 1899, Jonathan Cape, Penguin Random House.

A special thanks to the Batley RLFC stalwart, Bill Winner, who supplied various items of memorabilia which appear in the photos.

All photographs have been acknowledged wherever possible. If credit to the copyright has, inadvertently, not been obtained, it is entirely unintentional.

John Roe
Terry Swift
Ken Pearson
Craig Lingard
March 2020

Foreword

John Kear

It is with a great deal of pride that I write the foreword for this book about a club I was privileged to work for, while also being aware of its great history and central social contribution within the community. Batley Bulldogs RLFC, as it is now known, has been of massive importance to the game of rugby league: a founding member in 1895; winners of the inaugural Challenge Cup in 1897 and still playing out of a ground, Mount Pleasant, which is the second oldest in the game.

The club has had many ups and downs but has always held great importance and influence for the development of this great game and people within it. It has also been of even greater importance locally, as readers will come to realise.

Nowadays Batley is an established Championship set-up run in a vastly superior way to many of its contemporaries and is still central to the town's identity, all of which should give everyone connected with the club cause for great pride.

My connections with the place go back to making my professional debut in the Castleford 'A' Team in 1976 when Batley were the opposition, and my first ever application for a head coach's job in the late 1980s. Unfortunately, I didn't get the role but more than made up for it when I eventually did become head coach in 2011.

There is a lovely little story to go with that appointment that I think typifies the uniqueness of Batley and the excellent people who are connected with it.

Foreword

My time in charge of Wakefield Trinity was coming to an end and I was feeling a little out of love with the game and some individuals within it. I was seriously thinking of having a go at rugby union or having a break from league when, while travelling to Wembley to commentate on the Challenge Cup final for the BBC, I received a phone call from a number I was unfamiliar with. Upon answering it I found myself swept away by an enthusiast who absolutely loved the club and virtually told me I was going to be the next head coach of Batley when Karl Harrison left for Halifax.

That person was Kevin Nicholas, who concluded the call by inviting my wife and I down to the Toulouse game the following week, which is when Kevin was at his brilliant best. He knew I would enjoy watching the game, but what he did was convince my wife, Dawn, that this move was just right at this time in my life and career. For that I will be eternally grateful to both Kevin and my wife as what followed was an absolutely enjoyable and successful five years.

Yes, we achieved on the field, the club's typical against all odds spirit getting us to a Championship Grand Final in 2013 before becoming top part-timers in British RL in 2016, thereby qualifying for the Middle 8s when we met teams like Leeds. However, it was the special relationship with the club and everyone involved with it that really sits in the memory. It became, as I am sure it is to many of the readers of this book, a club that I love.

That is why I am so proud to be asked to contribute to this book, and why I am proud to be associated with Batley. Good luck to Craig Lingard, John Roe, Terry Swift and Ken Pearson. With the tireless amount of work you have put in, this very important endeavour deserves to be a huge success.

John Kear, March 2020

Preface

The history of Batley Cricket, Athletic and Football Club, later known as Batley RLFC and more recently as Batley Bulldogs RLFC, is a very rich story which commences in 1880, though the cricket branch of the original club pre-dates the rugby football section.

Of course, the original rugby football club was established under the aegis of the Rugby Union, but fifteen years after the club's formation it severed links with the latter and joined the breakaway Northern Union that subsequently became the Rugby League. Consequently, Batley Bulldogs, the initial rugby club having been established in 1880, is one of the oldest rugby league clubs in the world and its ground is also amongst the oldest rugby league venues in the world. However, Batley Bulldogs' initial nickname, which is still used in some journalistic quarters, 'The Gallant Youths', was acquired prior to the 1895 schism.

As may be expected of a club with a long history, that history is replete with many remarkable characters. Current spectators will, of course, be more familiar with names such as Carl Gibson , Simon Wilson, Barry Eaton, Paul Storey, Neil Kellett, Glen Tomlinson, Paul Harrison and Craig Lingard, but the club's reputation in the annals of the history of the sport was established by men such as Tom Elliker, Herbert 'Dodger' Simms, Jack Goodall, Mark Shackleton, George Main, Wattie Davies, Jim Gath, Joe Oakland, Bob Spurr and then reinforced by the likes of Ike Fowler and Frank Gallagher. Inevitably, there are individuals like Bill Hudson, Bill Riches, John Etty, Jack Perry, George Palmer and Norman Field, all outstanding players in their own right, but whose careers at Batley yielded no medals.

To some extent the fortunes of Batley RLFC have run in parallel with economic development and decline. The club was established at a time of economic growth and the team's major successes were achieved whilst the town was still economically vibrant. As will be explored in subsequent chapters, the club had acquired all of its major trophies before the end of the 1920s and then did not win another trophy, a minor one, until 1998. The reception given to the players and the celebrations which occurred on each of the occasions that Batley won the Challenge Cup provide ample testimony of the importance of the club to its townspeople. The economic history of the town after the Second World War is essentially one of industrial decline, a period during which the once thriving textile industry gradually disappeared as mill after mill closed down. In terms of results, the 1950s, 1960s, 1970s and 1980s were very lean years during which, apart from some outstanding individual performances and a few unanticipated victories, there was little to cheer the loyal fans.

Like all other rugby league clubs, Batley was battered by the impact of World War 1 and then by the Depression in the 1930s, but the club, in spite of the loss of key players who were killed during the first World War, rode out the storm, recovering sufficiently to win the League Championship title in 1924. During the Second World War, having survived the Depression years, the club, through the extensive use of guest players, was able to participate in the War-time competition. In fact there are probably few, if any, clubs which made more extensive use of guest players than Batley 1939-1945.

From the early years to more recent times the club has occasionally been in the news for reasons other than the performance of the team on the field. Sometimes this was the result of a quarrel with the governing authorities, as was the case in 1886 when Batley were in dispute about the designated re-play date for the semi-final of the Yorkshire Challenge Cup. On other occasions it was the result of the behaviour of fans or the extra-curricular activities of both players and former players, and most famously, in the 1970s, as a consequence of an internal dispute between the board of directors and the Supporters' Club. In the early part of the twentieth century the licensing laws, which had been introduced during the First World War, were frequently the cause of negative publicity. In fact pubs themselves play a part in the history of Batley Rugby Football Club in so far as a significant number of players either ran pubs whilst they were playing for Batley or once their playing careers had ended. Moreover, in the early years, The Royal Hotel, Bradford Road, Batley, was effectively the club headquarters.

One very noticeable feature of the club's history, at least until the end of the 1970s when the estate was reduced, is the extent to which the its estate was used for a wide variety of activities, including Batley Show, political rallies, a military tournament, charity sports events, athletic competitions, schools' sports events, Lacrosse games and brass band contests. All of these activities provide a clear indication that Batley Rugby Football Club made a contribution to the local community over and above the staging of rugby matches, thereby weaving itself into the fabric of the town.

Batley's ground, as indicated above, one of the oldest in the world, has undergone several transformations since the newly formed rugby football club played its first official game at Mount Pleasant against Bradford Zingari in October

Preface

1880. Once the club had established itself as a formidable force, it looked to develop the ground, a covered stand being officially opened in 1913. Though the ground fell into a state of considerable disrepair in the 1960s and then again, to some extent in the 1980s, more recently there has been a considered and determined effort by the directors to ensure that the facilities are fit for the twenty first century. Very often the name of a single family is associated with individual clubs in a variety of sports and this is the case with Batley Rugby Football Club. Members of the Auty family, a local mill-owning family, not only played for Batley (Wilf, Herbert and Willie), but the patriarch, Joseph Auty, was instrumental in enabling Batley C.A. and F.C. to buy the ground in 1904. Given that Mr. Auty was a fervent opponent of the consumption of alcohol, his role had important consequences for the club.

One of the threads that run through the history of Batley Rugby Football Club is the struggle to balance the books. In spite of Batley's stunning success at the end of the nineteenth and the beginning of the twentieth century, it was not long before the club encountered financial difficulties and this pattern was repeated following the Championship triumph in 1924. Given the distinct lack of success from that point on, coupled with the subsequent economic decline of the region, it is hardly surprising that the club often struggled to keep its head above water. As will be seen, the club, and sometimes the municipality, appealed to the public for additional funds. Whilst the club's finances have, in recent years, been generally sound, the 'War Chest', introduced in 2017 and aimed only at fans, may be seen to be in the same tradition as the appeals in the past. Inevitably, tight financial constraints have, over the years, limited the club's ability to hold on to its most talented players.

Since its establishment in 1926 the Batley Rugby League Supporters' Club has played an important role, particularly with regard to fund raising, in the history of Batley Rugby Football Club. In Chapter 7, there is an examination, based on the Supporters' Club minute book, of the activities of this organisation during the 1970s. More recently, BISSA – the Batley Independent Supporters' Squadbuilder Association, established in 2003 – has been active in raising money which can only be used for the acquisition and retention of players, a key function given what has been referenced above regarding the problems of retaining players.

In common with many other rugby league clubs, Batley RLFC owes a debt of gratitude to the local business community from which many directors and chairmen have emerged, ranging from mill owners to butchers and bakers. Some, such as Jackie Barritt, also made a contribution to the administration of the sport at national and county level. Particular mention should also be made of the late Ron Earnshaw, a former chairman in whose honour both a suite at the stadium and the Batley Bulldogs' Breakfast Club (Ron's Breakfast Club) are named. Ron worked tirelessly for Batley RLFC, both as a fan and a member of the board of directors.

Looking to the future, one of the most pressing problems faced by Batley Bulldogs is the shrinking fan base. Gone are the days when Batley could rely on regular crowds of two to three thousand. The demographic change which has taken place in the town, which now has a substantial British Asian population amongst which there is no tradition of supporting rugby league, makes it particularly difficult for the club to expand its fan base. Nonetheless, what can be guaranteed is that the dedicated volunteers who do so much to assist Batley Bulldogs' directors and paid employees, will continue do all they can for the club that they love.

1

ORIGINS

Batley Rugby Football Club was established in 1880, in October 1880 to be precise, emerging as an attachment to the Batley Cricket Club which had been officially set up in 1863. The story of its inception is a tale of dispute and controversy at a local level, but before we get there it is worth reflecting on the wider context from which this venerable rugby football club emerged.

The nineteenth century in Britain, and elsewhere, was a century of substantial social, economic and political change, though not for the most part linked to revolutionary activity. The Reform Acts of 1832 and 1867, The Chartist Movement of the 1840s and the Secret Ballot Act in 1872 contributed to the development of a political system more representative of the population, though still considerably short of democratic. Nonetheless, more male individuals became involved in decisions directly affecting their own lives. In this respect the genie was out of the bottle and could not be put back. Such a development was, arguably, to have important consequences towards the end of the century when the Rugby Union clubs in the north took the momentous decision to break away from the main body and form the Northern Union.

The 1800s was also when towns like Batley grew and prospered, in Batley's case primarily as a consequence of the ingenuity of Benjamin Law and the Parr family, the people who developed the processes for the manufacture of Shoddy and Mungo respectively, though the rapid growth resulted in considerable hardship for the majority of the population and prosperity for the few. The importance of these two closely related methods of cloth production for the growth of Batley cannot be overstated. They provided Batley and its close neighbour, Dewsbury, with a means by which they could exploit the increasing demand for textiles without having to compete directly with the manufacturers of higher grade products in Bradford and Huddersfield. In other words Batley was able to establish its niche in the market, admittedly as a consequence of manufacturing a cloth whose name became a synonym for substandard!

By the mid-nineteenth century the growth of the town and its allied economic activity was a subject of interest beyond the confines of Batley, as the following newspaper reports indicate:

POPULATION OF BATLEY

In our report of the proceedings connected with the opening of the Leeds and Dewsbury Railway, given in the Intelligencer *of the 5th inst., it was stated that the population of the township of Batley was 4,831.*

A correspondent requests us to state, "as an act of justice to the town", that the population in 1841 was 7,880, and that since then "it has greatly increased so that it may now be confidently returned at 10,000."

Our correspondent adds that there are "18 woollen mills in the township employing 570 horse-power."

The Leeds Intelligencer August 19th 1848

TRADE OF BATLEY

"We trust, ere long, to announce a brisk trade here; very large quantities of goods, which have been accumulating in the warehouses, we understand, have been disposed of. We hope our anticipations may be realised, for great distress has prevailed in this locality from scarcity of labour."

The Leeds Times May 6th 1848

The report from the *Leeds Times* highlights a key feature of economic growth, a demand for, coupled with concern about a shortage of, labour whilst the correspondent in the Leeds Intelligencer attests to a burgeoning pride in the economic significance of Batley. The writer is ever keen to demonstrate that the town is making its mark amidst the surrounding industrial activity.

Consequently, it was quite natural that local residents in a town such as Batley would wish to signal its growing significance through the establishment of a cricket club named after the town. Sporting activities, then as now, are means through which towns and cities can enhance their prestige, thereby attracting potential investors in the local economic activity. Batley Cricket Club was officially founded in 1863, emerging from the Prince of Wales Cricket Club. However, there is reference to a cricket club described as Batley Cricket Club as early as 1850:

On Monday last, cricket lovers had a high day's sport, it being the appointed day for the contest betwixt the Morley first eleven – full name Morley "Dartmouth" Cricket Club, and Batley Cricket Club first eleven, played at the ground near to the Dartmouth Arms, amidst a large concourse of spectators"

Leeds Intelligencer, June 22nd 1850

Origins

Of course it may be that the description of Morley's opponents as Batley Cricket Club is simply the result of imprecise journalism, the team merely coming from Batley rather than bearing that official title. Nonetheless, the reference to the "first eleven" does at least suggest that there was a vibrant cricket club in Batley as early as 1850, prior to the official establishment of Batley Cricket Club. Contemporary reports suggest that this new club quickly flourished and within a few years was capable of taking on and defeating the best teams in the county. The match between Batley and Lascelles Hall, which Batley won by 124 runs was covered thus by the *Dewsbury Reporter* 25th September 1869:

The above match was played on the Batley ground on Monday, and as it was a feast a large number of spectators met to witness the first treat they have had to see their town club pitted against what is considered the best in the county.

Between 1863 and 1880, the year in which Batley Cricket Club incorporated a rugby football section, the club became an integral part of the town and its associated institutions, its reputation known within the county. One year after Batley had been made a Municipal Borough, the proceedings of the "Annual Dinner of the Batley Cricket Club" were recorded in the *Dewsbury Reporter* November 13th 1869:

Our friends of the bat and ball held their annual supper on Wednesday night, the place of the rendezvous being the Talbot Hotel, New Road Side,. About seventy gentlemen sat down to a well spread table. Mr. Isaac Colbeck took the chair. There were members of the Town Council and others.

The report showed that the playing members had been very successful during the year, the first eleven having lost only two matches. There was a balance of £9. 10s 6d. The report was accepted, then loyal and patriotic toasts were given.

The ambitions and enterprise of the newly created municipal borough were fully reflected in the activities of the Batley Cricket Club during the period 1863-1880, which saw adverts placed in the *Sporting Life* and the *Yorkshire Post* in attempts to recruit a fast bowler, the employment of professional cricketers and the staging of significant matches at the cricket ground. In September 1872 a United North of England Eleven played against a Batley and District team at the Batley Cricket Club ground at the bottom of Howley ruins (the move to Mount Pleasant had not yet been made), whilst in September 1875 the opposition this time was a Yorkshire County Eleven. However, the icing on the cake came in June 1878 when a Batley and District team took on an Australian Eleven in a match which in the words of the *Bradford Telegraph* June 11th 1878 "excited a great deal of public interest on account of the opportunity that is being given during the holiday season to the lovers of cricket in this part of Yorkshire, to see one of the finest teams of cricketers judging from previous performances, the world has ever produced."

The staging of this game of cricket represented a considerable coup for the Batley Cricket Club, just two years before it expanded by adding a rugby football section. The significance of this fixture should not be underestimated, taking place as it did only one year after the very first test match between England and Australia at the Melbourne Cricket Ground. It is quite remarkable that the cricket club of a relatively small town should be able to stage a match against an Australian team composed of many of the players who had appeared in that first test. That the Batley team lost is much less surprising than that the match was played in the first place. The club was, as had been claimed by one speaker at the Annual Dinner in 1874, "one about which the people of Batley could boast." (*Huddersfield Daily Chronicle*, 9th November 1874). Moreover, by 1897 the people of Batley would have even more to boast about in connection with Batley Cricket, Athletic and Football Club, only this time it was with regard to the achievements of the Rugby Football section which had, by then, roundly eclipsed those of the Batley Cricket Club.

However, it would be remiss to create the impression that these early years of Batley Cricket Club were trouble free. A report in the *Huddersfield Daily Chronicle*, November 19th 1877, about the Batley Cricket Club Annual Dinner refers to particular financial difficulties faced by the club, as outlined by the Treasurer, who told those attending the Annual Dinner "If funds keep on decreasing at the same rate as the last two years, together with the diminished value of the refreshment tent, in all probability by the time our lease on the field has expired , which is in about two years time, we will be nearly at the verge of bankruptcy." It seems that these financial difficulties arose from a combination of a fall in gate money and problems associated with the collection of outstanding subscriptions. This is extremely instructive with regard to the subsequent history of Batley Rugby Football Club, which, as we shall see, was frequently dogged by financial problems, even shortly after its glory years 1897-1901. Of course, this is not unique to Batley and might now be seen as the perennial problem which faces the game of rugby league.

Batley Cricket Club had, as early as 1871, given consideration to the establishment of a rugby football section, but it was not until 1880 that this development actually occurred. As far as the Batley Cricket Club was concerned the key question was which of the various local rugby football clubs should be chosen to be incorporated into the club and so bear the official title of the Batley Rugby Football Club. In fact prior to 1880 there is some evidence that a local football (rugby) club styled itself as Batley Football Club, or at least was referred to as such by the *Dewsbury Reporter*, as distinct from Batley Athletic and Football Club, the team which was eventually chosen by Batley Cricket Club. On the 30th November 1878, the *Dewsbury Reporter* covers the following matches played on the same day the previous week: Batley Athletic and Football Club v Horbury; Batley Football Club v Liversedge Christchurch. It is not clear what happened to this proto-Batley club once Batley Athletic became the official Batley Football Club.

As indicated in the opening paragraph of this chapter, the circumstances in which Batley Athletic and Football Club came to be the official Batley Football Club is a tale of dispute and controversy. In 1880, the two pre-eminent rugby football teams in Batley were the aforementioned Batley Athletic and Football Club and the Batley Mountaineers. Indeed there is evidence of a vibrant rugby football culture in the town at the time. The *Leeds Times*, January 17th, 1880 lists four Batley teams playing on the same day: Batley Mountaineers; Batley Athletic; Staincliffe Britons and Batley Carr Trinity. A Batley team, which was probably Batley Athletic, featuring several names that would become well known in the future, J. Parker, T. Elliker and G. H. Wilks amongst them, played away against Thornes on 25th September 1880. This match, in which the Batley team was heavily defeated, was the subject of a substantial report in the *Yorkshire Post and Leeds Intelligencer*, 28th September 1880. Nonetheless, Batley Cricket Club, it seems, chose Batley Athletic as the team to represent the new football section of the club and their first game, the very first Batley match played at the new Mount Pleasant ground, was against Bradford Zingari on 2nd October 1880, a game which Batley won, though by exactly how many points it is, as a consequence of the somewhat obtuse scoring system, difficult to say. What we do know is that Bradford Zingari failed to score any points and, from the *Athletic News* 6th October 1880, that the team winning the toss, Bradford Zingari, began a trend that continues to the present day by choosing to play uphill in the first half. Batley's famous, or infamous slope, was a matter of record from the very first game at Mount Pleasant.

Thus the Batley Football Club had been officially launched and according to the *Leeds Times*, 16th October 1880, in a game against Leeds Parish Recreation, was already styling itself as Batley Cricket, Athletic and Football Club. However, this was by no means the end of the story of its inception. Batley Mountaineers, considering itself to be the pre-eminent team in Batley, took grave exception to the Batley Cricket Club's arbitrary selection of Batley Athletic as the team to represent the town and considered the challenge match between the two teams on 23rd October 1880 as the game that would decide which team should officially represent the town. As reported in the *Batley News* the following week "There was great excitement caused by the fact that the winner of this match was to hold the position of first club."Unfortunately the game was mired in controversy as a result of a disputed try, thus described in the local newspaper: "After some scrimmaging A. Parker got possession, made a run and placed the ball between the posts, but the referee called the ball back, but they would not bring it back, so all the spectators rushed in. The referee said there was four or five minutes left to play. The Mountaineers appeared on the field of play, but no more play took place. The referee called it a disputed game." The Mountaineers contention was that, knowing that Parker had knocked the ball on, they had made no effort to stop him and that Batley Athletic, fearing they would lose the match if play continued, had refused to return the ball.

The Batley Mountaineers seem to have been outmanoeuvred by Batley Athletic, whose strategy seemed to be based on the maxim "what they had they would hold". The Athletic, seemingly backed by the cricket club simply refused to play a return match, a decision which precipitated the following exchange of letters between the respective secretaries, as recorded in 'The Gallant Youths', Charles F Shaw, 1899:

Batley, October 28th 1880

Dear Sir – I received your letter and was sorry to learn that you were not going to play a return match. The communication was laid before our committee, and they were very sorry that you had come to this conclusion. They had nothing whatever to do with the disturbance which took place, it nearly all caused by your team getting a referee, and then, when he gave a decision against you, you refused to go on. He gave in as much against us as against you. If we had found the referee you would have had cause for complaint, but it all now rests with yourself, and if you don't think it wise to play us you will lose more than you will gain, because the gate money will do as much good for us as it will for you. I would not be party to such a proceeding. You can take it home to yourself. How would you have liked to have played at our ground with a good gate and then us refuse to play you in return, when you could be gainers by about a dozen pounds? Hoping you will lay this letter before the committee, and you can please yourself whether you play or not, but if you don't it will be worse for you. So no more from yours etc.

B. Smithson, Hon. Sec. Batley Mountaineers

Origins

November 2nd 1880

Sir, I laid your letter before our Committee last night, and on a motion being made that the minutes be confirmed as read, an amendment was moved that we confirm the minutes with the exception of the one relating to playing the return match with the Mountaineers. After a great deal of discussion the minutes were confirmed as read, so that we shall be unable to play the return match. I am requested to state several reasons why the committee refuse. The first is that your Captain was a party to encourage the breaking up of the game in case you thought a decision was given against you, and even if you were getting beat. I could give names, but it is thought best not to do so. Secondly, that both certain players and spectators threatened the referee, so that he dare not give his proper decision. Thirdly that your players used unnecessary violence when men were held down, one of our players especially was severely used by being bit and nipped badly. Fourthly, we were given to understand that before coming on to the field it was a made arrangement that if you were getting beaten the match was to be stopped. I could give many more reasons, but I think I have given plenty. I am sorry the match is not going to be played, so you will have the date open.

I remain yours respectfully.

Louis Hall, Hon. Sec. Batley Athletic

Batley Cricket Club stuck with Batley Athletic. Perhaps the Committee thought that of the two arguments put forward in this exchange of letters, the one from Batley Athletic was the more coherent. Thus the club officially became the Batley Cricket, Athletic and Football Club, a club whose achievements on the rugby football field would become widely known before the end of the nineteenth century. Let the official history of the team soon to be known as 'The Gallant Youths' commence.

TIMELINE: 1880s
UK and World Events

1880 – The word "boycott" enters the English language
        Gladstone becomes Prime Minister for the second
        time
1881 – Benjamin Disraeli dies aged 76
        Billy the Kid is shot and killed by Pat Garrett;
1882 – Death of Charles Darwin
        The first Christmas tree with electric lights is on
        sale in the USA
1883 – Death of Karl Marx
        The Volcano at Krakatoa erupts
1884 – The Third Parliamentary Reform Act is passed
        The Greenwich Meridian is created
1885 – The Statue of Liberty was placed on Liberty Island,
        New York
        The Rover Bicycle goes on sale – first bicycle with a
        chain drive
1886 – Karl Benz patents his first car, the three wheeled
        Motowagen
        First sale of Coca Cola, in Atlanta, Georgia, USA
1887 – Queen Victoria's Golden Jubilee
        Sherlock Holmes's first appearance in a story
1888 – John Boyd Dunlop patents his pneumatic tyre
        The 'Jack the Ripper' murders take place in London
1889 – The Eiffel Tower is opened in Paris
        Prevention of Cruelty to and Protection of Children
        Act introduced in the UK

2

EARLY YEARS: THE 1880s

Context

At this point it is worth taking a moment, briefly, to examine the sporting context into which the newly formed Batley rugby club emerged. It seems that the creation of a rugby section attached to the Batley Cricket Club was linked to an expansion of the handling game within Yorkshire, the first rugby clubs in England having only been officially established in the 1860s. The *Yorkshire Post and Leeds Intelligencer*, September 28th 1880, comments thus on what it regards as a welcome expansion of the game:

The wonderful advance of the Rugby game in Yorkshire during the past half dozen years, during which period players have increased from hundreds to thousands must have attracted the attention of all those who mark the progress of the sport. We can well remember the day – seems only a short time ago – when Yorkshire had only five clubs to do battle, viz: - Hull; Bradford; Huddersfield; Leeds and York. At that time a county contest was to be remembered, Durham and Lancashire being the only County games played......
......The attendance of the public, too, on such occasions was meagre, the notion being that football was an excessively rough and violent amusement. But the game slowly and surely advanced , and

the formation of the Yorkshire CFC, which offered the Challenge Cup, made football a recognised Institution. Excited and enthusiastic crowds from most towns and villages followed on.

Whilst we might consider the claim about "most towns and villages" a typical piece of journalistic hyperbole, it is clear that Batley C.A. and F.C. joined a vibrant Yorkshire rugby culture in 1880.The reference to the sport as "an excessively rough and violent amusement" will, with regard to the history of the club pre-World War 1, prove to be extremely prophetic.

One particular feature of the game of rugby which stands out at this stage of its development is the opaque nature of the scoring system which, with its combination of tries, conversions, touchdowns and minor points, sometimes makes it difficult to work out the final score. What is clear is the origin of the term conversion with regard to a kick at goal. A try's value was only realised and converted into actual points if the ensuing kick at goal was successful. It must be remembered that the sport was still in its infant years and as such the rules were evolving. In this sense the evolution of the rules is not dissimilar to the evolution of languages. The more widely spoken a language is the more likely it is that the rules of its grammar will be simplified. There is, of course, a slight contradiction here in that rugby league, whose geographic reach and number of participants are both significantly smaller than those of rugby union, has a much simpler set of rules. However, we shall see that there are very particular reasons for this apparent anomaly.

The sport as a whole was evolving in the 1880s and, having developed as an offshoot of Association Football, seeking to establish a unique identity. This may be seen from an article in the *Leeds Mercury*, 21st November 1882 about the respective merits of round and oval footballs:

The Early Years

Mr. Vassall (present captain of the Oxford fifteen) states in his letter that at Cheltenham College the round ball was used for the rugby game with the utmost success for several seasons. This is a matter in which experience is decidedly to be preferred to theoretical arguments, and it is hardly likely that clubs will bind themselves one way or another without trying both systems, then judging their comparative methods. The subject is worthy of ventilation, for with many the origin of the oval ball is enveloped in mystery, and its adoption has merely been from accident of education and practice.

Two systems of Rugby Football cannot, however, be kept on foot so as to permit the exchange of matches among clubs in the Union, and it is therefore necessary that the projected change (to the oval ball), if adopted by the majority, should be universally accepted, unless a split in the Rugby camp is to be permitted to take place.

It is fascinating to note that an early split in the Rugby Union might have occurred as a consequence of a debate about the most appropriate shape of the ball, a debate which revolved around aesthetics and utility, in contrast to the subsequent split which had its roots in issues linked to raw economics and class divisions.

One early aspect of the reporting of the game of rugby, an aspect that is doubtless not unique to rugby, is the inconsistency with regard to the spelling of players' surnames. This is particularly noticeable in connection with the early history of Batley C.A. and F.C., and it is not necessarily a feature of the reporting of the club's exploits which has improved over the years. Whenever there is an opportunity for an alternative letter to be used within a name, a letter to be added to or subtracted from a name, it is virtually guaranteed that it will be done. Thus in the early years there is Radcliffe/Ratcliffe, Wilks/Wilkes, Simms/Sims, Sykes/ Sikes, Whitaker/Whittaker, Hirst/Hurst and several other examples. This tendency reached its apotheosis in the 1970s when Steve Grinhaff's name (admittedly a slightly unusual spelling) was transmuted into Grin Offenstein!

The evolution of Batley C.A. and F.C.

Batley's very first home game at Mount Pleasant, against Bradford Zingari, has already been referenced, but the team's first fixture, one which turned out to be a baptism of fire, took place the previous week at Thornes. In short, Batley were thrashed, nilled in fact. Thornes amassed three goals, one disputed goal, five tries and fifteen touchdowns; an inauspicious start, indeed. The *Yorkshire Post and Leeds Intelligencer*, 28th September 1880, furnished quite a detailed report of the match, from which the following is an extract referring to a period during the first half:

For the next ten minutes the ball was within the visitors' quarters, and during that time they were obliged to touch-down twice. A free kick was obtained, and the Batley men following the ball up well, it was for the first time carried within the territory of the Thornes players. It was, however, quickly returned after an exciting struggle and another touchdown obtained by Thornes. Evans scored a try, but it was disputed by Batley, and the home team gave way.

Batley may have been soundly beaten in their first official fixture, but the final sentence of the above extract suggests that the match was played in a friendly spirit, in sharp contrast to some future battles.

As might be expected in connection with a club which had only been officially formed at the beginning of October 1880, Batley had no players featuring in the County Trial

Match which took place on 6th November 1880, even though the team contained such luminaries as Tom Elliker and Jacob Parker. The *Yorkshire Post and Leeds Intelligencer*, 29th October 1880 states that the opposing teams for the County Trial Match contained players from Halifax, Wakefield Trinity, Dewsbury, Huddersfield, Heckmondwike and Bradford Rangers. It is interesting to note that at this point Batley's local neighbours had stolen a march on them. However, this relative obscurity was not to last long because by 19th November 1880 the *Leeds Mercury* is able to report that:

In celebration of his approaching wedding Mr. H W T Garnett, the popular captain of the Yorkshire County Football Club, was entertained at dinner at the Griffin Hotel, Leeds on Wednesday evening and was presented with a handsome testimonial subscribed to by sixteen of the principal clubs in the county.

Batley FC was one of the sixteen clubs specifically mentioned as having contributed to the purchase of the solid silver salver which was presented to Mr.Garnett. It was not long before Batley CAFC, though the full title of the club was not always used, was making its mark within the Yorkshire region. The *Leeds Times*, Saturday 15th January 1881, records that the previous week Batley had beaten Huddersfield Rangers 13-1 at Batley, though the *Yorkshire Post and Leeds Intelligencer*, 11th January 1881 is more precise in listing the result as "one goal, five tries and thirteen minor points to one dead ball." The same edition of this newspaper adds that "The visitors, who played a grand uphill game, were completely overmatched, both in the loose and packed scrimmages, the heavier weight of the home team enabling them to carry all of the scrimmages."

It was in January 1881 that Batley first flexed its

muscles in the Yorkshire Challenge Cup, beating Harrogate in the first round. As Brian Cartwright noted in *A Ton' Full of Memories*, the team members were afforded a rousing welcome in the shape of a brass band playing "See the Conquering Heroes Come", when they arrived at Batley railway station. This was the first, but by no means the last time, that the team would be greeted by enthusiastic locals in the wake of an important victory. Unfortunately, Batley were unable to overcome Halifax in the second round, so their initial experience in this competition was short lived. Nonetheless, Batley had laid down a marker and signalled that they were ready to compete against the top clubs in the county.

Taken as a whole, Batley's first season as a rugby football club could be regarded as a successful one. Seventy seven percent of the 26 games played were won or drawn and the only points category in which their opponents outscored them was that of minor points. The Royal Hotel on Bradford Road was an important reference point for the club in the early years as it housed the changing rooms and was used as the location for the Annual General Meeting. The *Dewsbury Reporter*, April 22nd 1882 noted that:

The General Meeting of Batley Cricket and Athletic Club took place at the Royal Hotel, Bradford Road, on Monday evening. There was a large attendance. After voting for a new Committee the members were given details by the Secretary.

According to the above newspaper, "the meeting recognised the great success of the football section" and it was decided that the latter should have its own Financial Secretary. This development is not without significance, indicating, as it does, that the decision to add a football section to the cricket club had been vindicated. The football arm of the club was clearly adding value to the institution as a whole.

It was also in this early period that Herbert 'Dodger' Simms emerged as a key talent in the Batley squad. Though slight, Simms, as his nickname suggests was an elusive runner with the ball, but also one who could select and execute a killer pass which gave one of his teammates the opportunity to break through the opponent's defence. In the early and mid-1880s, report after report in a swathe of newspapers including the *Yorkshire Post, Leeds Mercury, Hull Daily Mail, Huddersfield Daily Chronicle* and *York Herald* amongst others, attests to the individual skills demonstrated by 'Dodger' Simms whenever he took to the field. His reputation as a unique player was sealed by his performance in a charity game in 1889 when he single-handedly took on a team of nine players and beat them. This is how it was covered in the *Reporter* 22nd June 1889:

On Tuesday a novel football match was played on the Batley C.A. and F.C. Ground between Simms, the well-known footballer, commonly called "the little dodger," and nine carriers from Carlinghow, for the benefit of Batley Cottage Hospital. Much interest was taken in the game and £6 10s was realised for the benefit of the institution. The result of the match was as follows – Simms four goals, two tries; carriers four goals, one try and five minors.

However, this novel feat along with his other on-the-field exploits was not the only reason 'Dodger' Simms appeared in the press. Later that same year Simms fell foul of the law. As will subsequently be revealed, he would later be in good company, since the same fate befell a number of other well known Batley players in the not too distant future. On

November 16th, 1889, under the headline "A Football Player Charged Under The Betting Act", the *Sportsman* reported that:

Yesterday at Batley, Herbert Simms, a prominent member of the Batley Football Club, who assisted his county several times last season, was charged with allowing his house, the Bull and Butcher Inn, Batley, to be used for betting.

Isaac Tolson, a bookmaker, and Wm. Jowett were charged with aiding and abetting Simms. The evidence for the prosecution was that three policemen came from Leeds and Shipley on the 4th, as detectives in plain clothes, and visited several public houses, taking notes of what was going on. Whilst in the defendant's house they saw Fawcett make a bet of 6 shillings with Tolson on a certain horse, and the latter booked the bet. They also saw three other bets made in the house.

The landlord was away at the time, but his wife was present. For the defence several witnesses denied point blank that any betting took place, and stated that placards were in the rooms prohibiting betting.

The bench found the charges proved, and fined Simms 2 pounds and costs, and the defendants 10 shillings and costs.

This was, of course, at a time when, long before off course betting was legalised in the 1960s, public houses and working men's social clubs were the obvious locations for illegal betting. Doubtless the case provided unwelcome publicity for Batley C.A. and F. C., but "Dodger" Simms would hardly have been the only publican whose premises were used for betting.

Aside from such diversions, Simms, along with players such as Elliker, Jacob Parker, Haslam, Whitaker and Ineson, raised the profile of the club during the 1880s. In July 1882, making use of the close season, Batley entered a six-a-side competition held at Wakefield United Cricket Club. The *Leeds Times*, 8th July 1882, informs us that six players from the Batley team took on six of the Thornes first team, the holders of the Yorkshire Challenge Cup. In the words of the *Leeds Times:* "After a well-fought struggle the Batley team defeated the holders of the Challenge Cup." This indicates that Batley meant business. Involvement in a competition in July demonstrates that the club was both serious about its preparations for the coming season and capable of taking on and beating the best the county could offer.

It was not only on the field that the club was making its mark, but also with regard to the administration of the game. On 5th June 1883, as reported in the *Bradford Daily Telegraph*, 6th June 1883, Batley Football Club contributed to a discussion, involving representatives from various football clubs in Yorkshire, which took place at the Commercial Hotel, Bradford, regarding plans for the "better administration of football affairs in Yorkshire." The idea seems to have been the establishment of a Yorkshire Rugby Union in order to represent and safeguard the interests of the rugby football clubs in Yorkshire. Batley sent no representative to the meeting but, according to the *Bradford Daily Telegraph*:

A letter was read from the Secretary to the Batley Football Club, stating that whilst the club was firmly of the opinion that the County Committee should be elective, they could not go to the extreme length of supporting a rival county organisation.

This example is instructive for two principal reasons. In the first instance it demonstrates that, within three years of its inception, Batley Football Club was not content to sit on the sidelines, but was ready to make an active contribution to the development of the game by getting involved in an important discussion about how the affairs of sport were run at the regional level. Secondly, the essence of this discussion appears to prefigure the tensions which came to a head in the following decade, leading ultimately to the formation of the Northern Union. In this instance, Batley C.A. and F.C appears to be backing the existing authority, though twelve years hence that position would be reversed.

1883 was an important year for both the cricket and football sections of the club. In addition to what has already been noted, a county cricket match between Yorkshire and a combined Lancashire and Notts team was staged at Batley C.A. and F.C's ground 17th – 19th September of this year, as reported in the *Sheffield Daily Telegraph* 25th September 1883. The choice of Batley as a venue for a county cricket match is a clear indication that the cricket section of the club had quite a high profile, one which could only have been beneficial for the club as a whole. This impression is reinforced by another article in the same edition of the *Sheffield Daily Telegraph*, an article which describes the welcome afforded Louis Hall, who had topped the Yorkshire batting averages, when he returned to Batley, his home town:

At the railway station the Temperance Band was waiting, and escorted the returned hero to the Batley Town Hall. An immense crowd of townspeople assembled and joined in the triumphant march.

This is reminiscent of the scenes following Batley Rugby Football Club's victory over Harrogate in 1881, demonstrating the importance of sporting achievements to the inhabitants of the town, achievements that reinforced each other through the combined nature of the Cricket, Athletic and Football Club, an institution which had become an integral part of the municipality. At this point it was the cricket section which had the higher profile, but it would not be long before the senior section began to be eclipsed by the achievements of its junior partner. Such was already being signalled by the autumn of 1883 when, at the end of October, two Batley players, Elliker and Hopkinson, were selected to play in the Yorkshire County Trial Match.

In December 1884, Jesus College, Cambridge, on tour in Yorkshire, opted to play Batley in a fixture which must have provided a considerable boost to the prestige of both the club and the municipality, most especially since the home team was victorious. Unsurprisingly, the local newspaper, the *Batley News*, 16th December 1884, carried a lengthy article describing the encounter, from which the following extracts have been selected:

The visit of the Cambridge (Jesus College) team who have had a pleasant tour of Yorkshire, was looked forward to in Batley with considerable interest, which received much enhancement from the fact that Bradford had had to "lick the dust" at the hands of the Cantabs. The prophets and wiseacres (at least some of them) ....foretold the downfall of the "shoddy town" club, and no small number of these and others who inwardly wished success to the 'Varsity men were present on the Purlwell ground to urge on the visitors by such ejaculations as "Well Done Cambridge" etc. Cambridge did well, but Batley did better, and no one can say anything, I presume, in detraction of the splendid victory of the home team without being compelled to admit that the visitors were overmatched.......

From a chat which the writer had after the match with Moline, one of the Cambridge players, the opinion was vouchsafed that Batley was a strong and speedy lot, but that the game as they played it was different, and rougher in character than what the college man had been accustomed to. "You know," said the gentleman, "it is not our game."

It is difficult to read these extracts without detecting a distinct whiff of the class divisions which became entrenched in Victorian England, divisions which were institutionalised in the sport of rugby when the split took place in 1895. From this date, and for many years into the future, the game played by Batley was most definitely not Cambridge University's game. On this occasion it seems that Batley did not have a friend in Jesus!

One of the features of Victorian England was the expansion of the rail network, a network which provided greater connectivity both within and between counties. Without the availability of rail travel, many of the fixtures of both rugby football and association football could not have taken place. Batley having been linked by rail with Manchester in 1848, the rugby team was able, on Saturday 27th December 1884, to play an away game against the Manchester Club, Bradford and Clayton, after which the players were hosted at a dinner by the Clayton Committee. The *Batley News and Birstall Advertiser*, January 3rd 1885, deeming this to mark an important development for Batley C.A. and F.C, carried a very lengthy article about the events, from which the following extracts are taken:

On the occasion of the match the Great Northern Railway ran an excursion to Manchester, by which the Batley team (who occupied a saloon carriage) and a large number of supporters proceeded......
.Arriving in Manchester at one o'clock (an hour and a quarter behind time), the Batley players were met by a wagonette, and having partaken of refreshment were driven to the ground of the Bradford and Clayton Club, which is in Ashton New Road, about three miles from the city.

At the conclusion of the match the players adjourned to

The Early Years

Brown's restaurant in Corporation Street, Manchester, where the Clayton Committee entertained them to a first-class dinner. The number present was between 50 & 60, which included friends of both teams.

....one may venture to say that in meeting the Bradford and Clayton Club (Manchester) on Saturday last, Batley received what would not be inaptly described as a right royal welcome. The good feeling shown and the hospitality afforded to the visitors was something which could not be but gratifying to any team, and the day will be remembered as one of the pleasantest in the club's season's engagements.

The report of this fixture also gives some indication of how far Batley had progressed since September 1880, in that the article makes it clear that Bradford and Clayton, an up and coming club, regarded this game as an opportunity for the team to benefit from playing against first-class opposition. In the after dinner speeches the Batley team is variously described as "formidable" and "second to none in Yorkshire." Allowing for some hyperbole on the part of the generous hosts, this was praise indeed for a club which had only been officially competing for four years.

The first trophy

A dozen years before Batley won the inaugural Challenge Cup, in April 1885 the club acquired its first trophy, the Yorkshire Challenge Cup. In the semi-final, 28th March 1885, Batley defeated the favourites, Bradford, in order to progress to the final against Manningham on Saturday 4th April. The *Wharfedale and Airedale Observer and Otley and Ilkley Guardian*, 2nd April 1885, in reporting Batley's semi-final victory not only lavished praise on the Batley team, but also used the term 'gallant youths' to describe the players. At this point the term was not as yet an official nickname, but was used in a more general sense, not just in relation to Batley's squad, to describe teams whose players were youthful. However, it would not be long before this description became Batley's official soubriquet. With regard to Batley's semi-final victory the aforementioned newspaper, having highlighted the telling contributions of Terry, Parker, Ineson, Haslam, Simms, Radcliffe and Naylor, concluded with the comment:

That the best team won there cannot be any doubt, and the gallant youths of Batley deserve nothing but praise – praise the most lavish and unstinted that can be bestowed.

Given the relative proximity of Wharfedale etc. to Bradford, it might be assumed that the natural bias of this newspaper would be in favour of the latter, in which case the above comment is even more significant. Equally, it could be that there was a natural resentment of the 'big city neighbour' in the more rural district of Wharfedale and Airedale, in which case lavish praise for Bradford's victorious opponents is less surprising. Nonetheless, Batley went on to win the final, which was played at Cardigan Fields, Leeds, on Saturday 4th April 1885, the match receiving extensive coverage in the *Bradford Daily Telegraph, Yorkshire Post* and, as might be expected, *Batley News and Birstall Advertiser*. All three news outlets attested to Batley's worthy victory, though not necessarily in unequivocal terms. The *Bradford Daily Telegraph*, 6th April 1885, reported that:

....Mr. G.E Hudson, president of the County Committee, ... said that all who had seen the match or who had watched the progress of the Batley Club throughout the competition would endorse his words when he said that throughout all these years the cup had

25

never been more honestly won or would be more worthily held by the club which had earned the right to its possession for the next twelve months.

The *Yorkshire Post*, 6th April, 1885, which provided a very detailed report of the match itself, charting in fine detail the back and forth nature of the game, was less than enthusiastic about Batley's general performance, but fulsome in its praise of the club's overall achievement and commitment to excellence:

The exhibition of football was a good one, the score showing that the result was no foregone conclusion. Victory fell to Batley, but they hardly played up to their reputation.... In the end, however, Batley won in gallant style, but only by minor points (8 – 2), a very close margin indeed.

There will be very few indeed who will begrudge Batley their well-won and richly deserved honours. A short time ago they were, comparatively speaking, unknown. Now, they have reached the very top of the ladder of fame. This marvellous advance has been brought about by assiduous practice – early and late. Each man has acquired in this way a sound knowledge of the game, and more particularly that part having reference to passing. Though very light, their teamwork is undeniably excellent.

Even Batley's local newspaper, the *Batley News and Birstall Advertiser*, 11th April, 1885, betrayed a slight sense of disappointment with the manner of the victory:

Now, as regards the match itself, ...I must confess to a sense of disappointment at the result – that is as far as the scoring goes. There seems to be something wanting in connection with Batley's victory and it is that neither goal nor try was obtained. Having been accustomed during the season to see Saturday's winning team run up major points, one is tempted (however wrongly it may be) to be dissatisfied with minor points only.

Nonetheless, the newspapers were united in their view that the final, as an event, had been a roaring success, both for the victors and the game of Rugby in Yorkshire, exciting interest not just in Batley and Bradford, but across the county as a whole and, as we shall see, even in the USA. The attendance at the Cardigan Fields, Leeds, exceeded expectations, the numbers boosted by the bright sunshine following several days of rain. The *Yorkshire Post*, 6th April, 1885, summed up the scene admirably, reinforcing along the way the importance of the railways in the development of rugby football as a competitive sport and, allowing for some exaggeration regarding the crowd size, the extent of its mass appeal in Yorkshire:

Long before the time announced for the commencement of hostilities, people began to turn their faces towards Kirkstall Road. All along the route the scene was very animated, and it was apparent the attendance would be enormous. Special trains were run from the various towns – from Bradford, Dewsbury, Batley, Wakefield etc. Inside the ground.... A couple of grandstands were filled to repletion, even the adjacent hills being covered with a thick mass of football-loving humanity. Altogether the spectators must have numbered quite 15,000.

Such was the interest in the match amongst the people of Batley that, as recorded in the *Batley News and Birstall Advertiser*, 11th April, 1885, special arrangements were made to accommodate the needs of those who were unable to travel to Leeds to watch the game:

The Early Years

Notwithstanding the large number of Batleyites who were present to witness the match, there was of course a majority who stayed at home, but who nevertheless were very anxious as to the result. Special arrangements had been made to keep all such absentees fully acquainted with the game as it proceeded, and to this end messages (telegraphic and per carrier pigeon) were sent to Batley direct from the field. Commercial Street throughout the whole afternoon was thronged by an anxious crowd eager to learn the state of affairs in regard to the winning of the Challenge Cup.

The excitement of the townsfolk of Batley at the prospect of winning the Yorkshire Challenge Cup was nothing compared to the celebrations which took place once the victory had been secured. In scenes that would be replicated in 1897, thousands gathered at the bottom of Hick Lane, along Station Road and even on the station platform, well in advance of the anticipated arrival of the team at Batley Station, in order to greet the returning heroes. The Batley Old Brass Band, stationed on the platform, blasted out a rendition of 'See the Conquering Hero Comes' as the train steamed into the station. It is tempting to suggest that this was the only tune they knew, given that it was played to serenade both the returning Louis Hall in 1883 and the first winners of the Rugby League Challenge Cup in 1897, though this is doubtless too harsh a judgement on a group of dedicated locals. However, this 'serenade' was nothing as compared to the deafening cheers which greeted the appearance of the team, cheers which continued as the horse-drawn waggonnettes transporting the players and the trophy, processed to the market place, passing ecstatic crowds of people along the way. As recorded in the 11th April edition of the *Batley News*, "the event continued to be the talk of the evening, and it was a late hour before the streets began to assume their wonted aspect."

As indicated earlier, the excitement generated by the final extended to the USA, or at least a tiny enclave within the USA. Quite remarkably the *Batley News and Birstall Advertiser*, 23rd May 1885, under the heading: **BATLEY MEN IN THE UNITED STATES – REJOICING OVER THE FOOTBALL VICTORY**, included the following:

Mr. C. Wilson of Manayunk (Philadelphia) writes us as follows:- "Dear Sir, your insertion of these few lines about our rejoicings will gratify many Yorkshire people residing in this neighbourhood. When we received the news of the victory of the invincible Batley Football Club over Manningham, in the final contest for the Yorkshire Challenge Cup, a number of us decided not to let the occasion pass without having a jovial meeting of the Manayunk Club, and lovers of football generally. We met on Thursday, the last day of April, at Wilson's Commercial Hotel, Manayunk, and partook of a supper, prepared in the good old Yorkshire style. When the cloth was withdrawn we all drank to 'The health, long life, and standing of the Batley Football Club,' and gave the toast musical honours. After this we conversed on the glorious victory of little Batley over all Yorkshire, and many of us wished we could drink a toast out of the coveted prize. The evening was spent most pleasantly, great enthusiasm being exhibited at the pluck and success of our gallant old friends."

In the 19th century Manayunk, a district in Philadelphia, Pennsylvania, was an important centre for textiles, this presumably being the reason for the presence of an ex-patriot community of people from Batley. It may be that these individuals were skilled weavers or warpers whose expertise being highly valued in the USA, had been lured there by the promise of a better life. Whatever the reason for their move to the United States, their attachment to the town and its rugby football club had been kept alive.

Building on success

On the back of their stunning success in the Yorkshire Challenge Cup, Batley, in the early part of the 1885-6 season, embarked on a mini-tour of Lancashire and South Wales, a tour that was referenced in both the *Leeds Mercury*, 19th September 1885 and the *Yorkshire Post*, 22nd September 1885. The former, in reporting on the game between Batley and West Lancashire and Border Town Union, highlights the fact that the Batley team turned out, for the first time, in white jerseys as opposed to their usual cerise and fawn. The *Yorkshire Post* drew attention to the nature of the opposition that Batley was due to encounter in South Wales:

The Batley team, after a much needed rest on Sunday, travelled on to Newport yesterday morning to meet the very powerful team connected with the Newport club, who had whipped up a strong team, and being the holders of the Welsh Challenge Cup much interest was manifest in the match.

In the event, Batley triumphed in both matches, though they failed to score a try against their Welsh opponents. However, it seems that the team suffered a slight dip in form in the very early part of this season as is indicated in the 'Football Notes' section of the *Yorkshire Post*, 17th October, 1885, in which there is a reference to what now appears to have become the team's official nickname:

A close and exciting game should also be witnessed at Batley, where the 'gallant youths' oppose Broughton for the first time. The Cup-

holders have not yet been seen at their best, the forwards lacking that dash which so characterised their actions twelve months ago. The past day or two has, however, seen them indulging in hard exercise, and we look to them to win the day.

However, it was the Yorkshire Challenge Cup which kick started a return to the form that had seen Batley lift the trophy for the first time in 1885. The following year, once again, Batley progressed to the semi-final stage where they encountered Halifax in a fixture that was to spark a controversy which led to a mass demonstration in Batley Market Square, a controversy which has links with the issue of 'broken time', the key issue which led to the formation of the Northern Union in 1895. On Saturday 3rd April 1896, Batley defeated Halifax in the semi-final but Halifax lodged an objection against the only try of the game, scored by Batley, claiming that as the referee had blown his whistle to signal an incidence of offside-play, the ball should have immediately become dead prior to the Batley try having been scored. The Yorkshire County Football Association Committee met on Monday 5th April 1886 and, having upheld the objection from Halifax, in spite of a disagreement between the touch judges and the referee as to whether offside-play had occurred, ruled that the match should be replayed at Huddersfield on Wednesday 7th April. This was not in any way acceptable to Mr. John Blackburn, the Batley representative of the County Committee, and Mr S. Tankard who, along with Mr. Blackburn, was representing Batley at this special hearing. The response of John Blackburn, as outlined in the *Batley News*, 8th April, 1886, is instructive with regard to the tensions that were beginning to build up within the sport:

The Early Years

*Mr. J. W. Blackburn then remarked that it was a certainty that the
Batley team would not play the match on Wednesday. If they played
the match at all it would be next Saturday, or they would forfeit the
cup. They had had two or three week-day matches and it was too
much to call upon the players to break time on another week-day
when it was not needed.*

In the end Batley forfeited the game, thereby resolving the
immediate problem, but the issue of "broken time" was
merely shelved, only to return with a vengeance in the
following decade. Moreover, in October 1886, Batley had their
revenge against Halifax, who had gone on to win the
Yorkshire Challenge Cup, beating them in a closely fought
game at Mount Pleasant. The *Yorkshire Post*, 18th October
1886, in reporting on the match, eulogised about Batley's
progress over the last few years:

*Batley during the past three years has developed itself in a
wonderful manner. From being a very ordinary lot of individuals,
they have by careful drill and practice, overcome the intricacies of
combined action. Science pure and simple has mainly contributed
to their many successes, and at the present time they are one of the
most perfectly drilled and scientific body of players in the country.*

Precisely what is meant by the use of the word "science" in
this context is not immediately clear, but it is perhaps safe to
assume that the journalist is drawing attention to
development of technical skills amongst the players, along
with an awareness of tactics within the team as a whole.

It was also in October 1886 that Tom Elliker, in a game
against Broughton, ended up playing for most of the second
half in his stockinged feet as a result of an objection to his
boots lodged by Batley's opponents. Elliker's performance

does not appear to have been adversely affected by this unusual restriction, though it appears that he refrained from kicking the ball, concentrating on his running and passing game. The *Bradford Daily Telegraph*, 1st February 1887, reported that Batley's ground had been chosen as the venue for a county game between Yorkshire and Surrey on 14th February 1887. The match report in the *Leeds Mercury*, 15th February 1887 notes that three Batley players, Bedford, Elliker and Jackson, played for Yorkshire on home soil, and by the late 1880s it was quite usual for members of the Batley team to be selected to play for the County. A less glamorous, though no less important feature of the development of the club was the creation of an "A" (reserve) team, a feature that was in place by early 1887, as may be detected from a brief match report in the *Yorkshire Post*, 1st February 1887, about a game between Normanton and Batley "A" team.

At the end of November 1887 Batley C.A. and F.C. embarked on a tour of Scotland, playing matches against Carlisle (en route), West of Scotland and Hawick, a tour that was covered in great detail by the *Batley News and Advertiser*, 3rd December 1887. The tour, which resulted in victories against Carlisle and Hawick and a draw with West of Scotland, was considered to be a great success. The *Batley News* highlighted the extent to which Carlisle supporters and players both enjoyed the game and appreciated the fact that the Batley team had taken the trouble to break their journey to Scotland in order to play this match:

The exhibition of the Batley men gave immense pleasure to all who had seen the game and Carlisle players afterwards were free in stating their opinion as to the fine passing, running and kicking of the backs. Several declared that they had been taught a lesson which in future they would themselves endeavour to imitate.

The Early Years

Mr. Westray, President of the Cumberland County Club, said the Batley players had that day given the spectators a grand exhibition of genuine and scientific football....

Mr. Westray said that Carlisle appreciated very much this visit of the Batley club, because they came not only in a friendly way, but without any financial consideration whatever.

The following year, on 10th December 1888, Batley faced the New Zealand Maoris in a game which ended as a draw. As might be expected, the encounter was an item of interest for the Yorkshire press with match reports appearing in the *York Herald* and *Leeds Mercury,* 11th December 1888, *Yorkshire Post,* 12th December 1888, and *Leeds Times* and *Batley News,* 15th December 1888. Clearly this was a major coup for the club, a fixture against an antipodean touring team which doubtless selected its matches carefully, the game being only one of two that the tourists played in Yorkshire (the other was against the Yorkshire County Team). The *Leeds Times* thought Batley did very well to obtain a draw:

Contrary to general expectations the Batley fixture ended in a draw, which was decidedly favourable to the Batley players.....

The *Leeds Mercury* and *Batley News* disagreed about the size of the crowd (the former said 6,000, the latter 4,000-5,000), but were in agreement about the enthusiastic nature of the spectators. The *Batley News* had the following observation:

....cheap trains brought a large number of people from outside districts to Mount Pleasant, the scene of the encounter. At the Royal Hotel, the headquarters of the Batley club, a large crowd assembled to witness the arrival of the visitors, who on turning out on the field were greeted with hearty cheering.

It is not difficult to imagine that the arrival of a Maori team in Batley in 1888 would, for many locals, have been a very exotic event.

Thus by the end of the decade, only ten years after the inception of the rugby football club, Batley had become a force to be reckoned with and a name that was known, in rugby circles, well beyond the confines of the county. Batley's fixtures , in the late 1880s, were being reported in the press in some unlikely places: *Birmingham Daily Post* and *Hartlepool Daily Mail*, 11th November 1889; *Dundee Courier and Argus*, 18th November 1889. Moreover, at the start of this final year of the decade *The Athletic News*, 14th January 1889, under the heading "GALLANT YOUTHS" AT BROUGHTON, confirmed that Batley's soubriquet was now official.

The Batley team, who are known by the above singular title…

However, in the future, this "title" was a source of irritation for some who were unaware of the precise origins of the nickname. The *Yorkshire Evening Post*, 9th April 1898, printed the following letter from a Mr. J. Kilburn, whose address is not given, but who was probably from Leeds:

Dear Old Ebor,
Will you kindly say in your Football Notes why it is that when one reads about a Batley match the Batley players are always alluded to as the gallant youths or gallant lads? Are they any more gallant than, say, the Hunslet or Leeds players? For it is rather singular that for years past on every conceivable occasion the papers always when mentioning the Batley team, speak of them as the gallant youths, and other grand titles, which they never think of applying to any other club...

'Old Ebor' replied, perhaps to the consternation of Mr. Kilburn, that the term originated from the mid-1880s when Batley had won their first trophy and had since become accepted as the team's official nickname, though he did acknowledge that, at least in its original usage, it was an expression of admiration.

Multi-purpose use of the ground

Throughout the 1880s Batley C.A. and F.C. allowed its estate to be used for a wide variety of activities, a practice that continued into the next century and beyond. In addition to the preaching of two sermons on the cricket field, August 1881, a nine-a-side football contest, August 1882, a Lacrosse match between Batley C.A.and F.C. and Leeds and a brass band contest, both in July 1884, the *Huddersfield Daily Chronicle*, 20th June 1881 reported the following:

The 4th annual festival of athletics, promoted for the benefit of Batley Cottage Hospital, was held in the New Batley Cricket Field, at Mount Pleasant, last Saturday, and was attended by no fewer than 5,000 people, many of whom were attracted from a distance to witness the Cumberland and Westmoreland Wrestling matches, which had been announced. There were no fewer than 270 entries for the several prizes given for sprint, long distance and bicycle racing etc.

TIMELINE: 1890s
UK and World Events

1890 – Otto von Bismarck, the German Chancellor, resigns
Vincent van Gogh commits suicide
1891 – The birth of Basketball
Death of Charles Stewart Parnell, the Irish Nationalist
1892 – Official opening of Ellis Island Immigration Station
Liverpool A.F.C. is founded
1893 – World's Fair opens in Chicago
The first meeting of the Independent Labour Party
1894 – Publication of *The Jungle Book* by Rudyard Kipling
Blackpool Tower is opened
1895 – Oscar Wilde is found guilty of gross indecency
The first slot machines are introduced, in the USA
1896 – The first Modern Olympic Games are held in Athens
The Lumiere Brothers project their films in London
1897 – The publication of Bram Stoker's *Dracula*
The Tate Gallery opens in London
1898 – The death of William Gladstone, aged 88
The Spanish – American War
1899 – Marconi transmits a radio signal across the English Channel
The Second Boer War begins

3

TOWARDS THE SCHISM AND THE GLORY YEARS: 1890-1900

The years 1890-1990 were truly momentous, both for Batley C.A. and F.C. and for the game of rugby as a whole. This was the decade during which the Northern Rugby Football Union broke away from the Rugby Football Union, creating the organisation which would become the Rugby Football League, as well as the one in which Batley won the inaugural Rugby League Challenge Cup and retained it the following year.

The early 1990s

As indicated in the previous chapter, by the beginning of the 1990s 'The Gallant Youths' had built a reputation which extended well beyond the confines of Yorkshire, a reputation that was to be both consolidated and enhanced during the following decade, as were the individual reputations of some of the team's players. The *Leeds Mercury*, 29th September 1890, in a report on a game between Leeds Parish Church and Batley, made specific reference to Herbert Simms, alluding to the origins of his nickname "Dodger": "....and then Naylor passed to the renowned Simms, who executed one of his dodgy runs to the centre .... Simms ran in a grand try just prior to the conclusion...." The same player's all round athletic prowess was noted in the *Huddersfield Daily Chronicle*, 14th July 1891, in a report about Slaithwaite Cricket Club's annual sports competition: "The sprint race ended in a dead heat between Simms, the well-known Batley football player and Bailey, of Bailcliffe Bridge...." The York edition of the *Yorkshire Herald*, 5th February 1891, has a report of a game between Batley and Owens College (precursor to Manchester University), a prestigious fixture which indicates that Batley C.A. and F.C. was a well regarded outfit.

Once again, in late January 1892, Batley embarked on a tour of South Wales, a tour in which they lost to Llanelli and beat both Penygraig and Cardiff Harlequins, the proceedings being covered in the *London Evening Standard*, *Yorkshire Evening Post*, *South Wales Daily News* and, as might be expected, *Batley News*. Notwithstanding some eccentric spellings of the Batley players' names, the *South Wales Daily News*, 27th January 1892, provided a very detailed and complimentary report about the match between Cardiff Harlequins and Batley:

From start to finish the game was brimful of incident, and from the spectators' point of view one of the most interesting exhibitions of football seen in the district for some time. Fast and exciting, at no time was there anything verging on rough play. Both sides were in good humour, the visitors were mightily pleased with themselves, while the 'Quins took their defeat like true sportsmen. There can be no doubt that the best team won. Quite early in the game it was clearly seen that the Batley forwards were a formidable lot....

Given the positive impact that Batley made in South Wales, it is perhaps no surprise that the *South Wales Daily News*, 1st February 1892, contained a report of Batley's home game against Huddersfield on 30th January 1892, whilst the *Batley News*, 30th January 1892, was certain that, in spite of the loss to Llanelli, the tour had been an unmitigated success:

The tour of the Batley F.C. has this season been one of the most successful yet promoted. The party left Batley last Friday morning shortly before ten, and arrived at Swansea about eight the same evening. On Saturday they met and succumbed to the Llanelly Fifteen, whose prowess is well known in South Wales. On the Monday following the "towerers" opposed Penygraig and succeeded in chalking a victory. The contingent then moved their belongings to the Grand Hotel, Cardiff, and next day defeated Cardiff Harlequins, who are supposed to be one of the best teams in Wales. On the whole a very enjoyable time has been spent, and on their return every member of the party expressed their pleasure at having been afforded such an outing.

Whilst it might be expected that Batley's tour of South Wales would have been covered in the *South Wales Daily News*, the same would not be true of the *London Evening Standard*, yet in addition to reporting on Batley's game against Cardiff Harlequins (*L.E.S.* 27th January 1892), this newspaper also included reports about Batley v Halifax (*L.E.S.* 19th October 1892) and Batley v Manningham (*L.E.S.* 9th November 1892). With regard to the former, Batley's home game against Halifax was the only match in the Yorkshire Senior Club Competition that was reported on in this edition of the *London Evening Standard*, which even went as far as referring to both the size of the crowd and the fact that Batley won in spite of having to play uphill in the second half. It seems that the significance of the Mount's legendary slope was already known in the capital. Moreover, as there is a report in the same edition about an association football match between

Millwall and Sheffield United, in which a crowd figure is also given, it appears that there was a larger crowd at Batley's game than at Millwall's ground.

It is not the purpose of this book to provide endless details of dry statistics which chart the weekly progress of the team, as those details can be found elsewhere, primarily on the heritage website. However, there are some details and statistics relating to the early 1890s that are worthy of attention. In April 1893, once again Batley reached the final of the Yorkshire Challenge Cup, but unfortunately on this occasion the team lost 8-2 to Halifax. Nonetheless, the *Yorkshire Evening Post*, 22nd April 1893, supplied a substantial amount of information about each individual member of the Batley team. Below is a table which charts the age, weight and height of each player:

Name	Age	Weight	Height
Ike Shaw	26	10st 7lbs	5ft 4.5ins
Joe Naylor	26	11st 0lbs	5ft 6.5ins
J.B. Goodall	19	11st 4lbs	5ft 6.5ins
H. Simms	34	10st 4lbs	5ft 4.5ins
Jim Naylor	28	12st 3lbs	5ft 7.5ins
Tom Elliker	32	11st 3lbs	5ft 7.5ins
F.W. Lowrie	24	14st 0lbs	5ft 11.5ins
M. Shackleton	22	12st 7lbs	5ft 11.5ins
A. Thornton	26	13st 7lbs	5ft 11ins
W. Farrar	23	11st 12lbs	5ft 8.5ins
J.A. Haigh	22	11st 7lbs	5ft 8.5ins
J. Oldfield	28	11st 7lbs	5ft 6ins
W. Scott	20	12st 2lbs	5ft 10ins
Chas Squires	22	12st 7lbs	5ft 6.5ins
C. Stubley	22	12st 2lbs	5ft 6.5ins

Towards the Schism

We can thus calculate from statistics that the average age of the players was 25, the average weight was 11st 12lbs and the average height was 5ft 7.5ins. By comparison with their counterparts in the modern game of rugby league these players were small, but of course the players of today have benefited from the wider availability of nutritious food in addition to developments in the science of nutrition. However, the average age of the team confirms what is still true today, that, with regard to active participation in the sport, rugby league is a young man's game.

One of the team's two elder statesmen, Tom Elliker, was given a very generous write-up which highlighted his influential role in the club's development along with his overall commitment to fair play:

"Good old" Tom Elliker is one of the evergreens, who in years gone by assisted in earning the title of 'gallant youths'. The old time passing which made Batley so famous, emanated from this old stager, who yet possesses all his old time dash, and throws the ball as of yore. It can never be said that Elliker descends to any mean trickery, but always endeavours to play the game as it should be played. It will be some 13 years ago since he put on the war paint and joined a small lot somewhere in the neighbourhood of his native home. Being always well up in athletics he eventually drafted into the Batley ranks. At one period in his career he played for Leeds St. John's, and afterwards assisted Bramley. Returning to his old love, however, two seasons ago, he has figured with Batley ever since.

Though Batley went on to lose the final, the same edition of the *Yorkshire Evening Post* (22nd April, 1893) noted that:

The executive of the 'gallant youths' club was one of the first to recognise the necessity for the institution of a Senior Competition, and the success which has attended that venture is now a matter of common knowledge.... One matter of which the Batley committee and supporters are very proud is the fact that during the season very few extra men have been played and that to all intents and purposes the team which represented the club today was the same which had done duty through a most arduous season.

The early 1890s also saw the emergence of players who subsequently became famous as members of the all conquering team of the late 1890s, players such as J.B. Goodall, F.W. Lowrie, J. Naylor, A. Garner and Mark Shackleton, the last of whom went on to make a name for himself as one of the club's trainers. "Dodger" Simms, coming towards the end of his illustrious career, would not feature in the "glory" years, but he had already established his place in the history of Batley C.A. and F.C. Prior to the schism in 1895, the club continued to supply players for the Yorkshire County team, F.W. Lowrie, J.B.Goodall and Joe and Jim Naylor amongst them. The Royal Hotel continued to be an important base for the club, the venue for the annual dinner. The honoured guest at the dinner in 1890 was the President of the Yorkshire Rugby Union who, according to The *Yorkshire Herald*, 15th October 1890, addressed an issue which had caused some tension within the national game:

The annual dinner of the Batley Football Club was held at the Royal Hotel, Batley, last night and the Rev. F. Marshall, President of the Yorkshire Rugby Union, who was the guest of the evening, made references to the County Championship question. The Rev. gentleman said that respecting the recent Yorkshire victory at the Rugby Union in London he did not wish his hearers to think that victory was altogether a Yorkshire one. It was a victory for truth and justice. Yorkshire was fighting for the cause of right, and anything more detrimental to the game than setting northern counties against southern counties he could not imagine.

Though the cause of this tension in 1890 related to the restructuring of the County Championship rather than any issues associated with "broken" time, it is clear that the differences of opinion divided along a north south line, a division that was to be much more clearly and narrowly delineated in the not too distant future.

Going Forward

As befitted a club which had achieved fairly rapid success and was both forward looking and ambitious in its approach to the development of the game, Batley C.A. and F.C. invested in improvements to the ground in 1894. The *Yorkshire Evening Post*, 25th April 1894, in listing details of the club's balance sheet reveals that one hundred and forty one pounds and ten shillings had been spent on the purchase and fixing of a new stand, a stand which had been used at the Yorkshire Agricultural Show in Dewsbury. It is also worth noting that the income from the Football section of the club now outstripped the income from the Cricket section by a factor of five to one. A report in the above newspaper, 25th April 1895, reinforced the picture of a club that was not content to stand still:

The annual general meeting of the Batley Cricket and Football Club was held last night. The report showed the football season had been fairly prosperous. A balance due to the bank of four hundred and fourteen pounds. Many improvements have been made in the field at Mount Pleasant, giving more accommodation and convenience to playing members and public.

As indicated at the end of the previous chapter, the club's estate was, during the 1880s, used for a variety of activities, a practice which continued into the next century and beyond. In 1896 the very first "Batley Show" was held at Mount Pleasant, an event which in addition to becoming a fixture in the annual local calendar for many years to come, also served to remind the inhabitants of a predominantly industrial town of its agricultural heritage and the continuing links between industry and agriculture. The *Leeds Mercury*, 1st June 1896, in a lengthy article recording the event, attested to both its ambition and popularity.

The Batley and District Agricultural Society held their first annual show on Saturday afternoon, in the football field at Mount Pleasant. The number and quality of the entries, and the large attendance of the public, must have been very gratifying to the officials of the new Society.

For several years there has been a May-day horse procession in the town, and it is out of that movement that the present and more ambitious project of holding every year a full-fledged exhibition of horses, cattle, dogs, pigeons and rabbits has grown....

There were several very neat turnouts in the classes for local tradesmen, and admirable specimens of the heavy draught horses which are so extensively used in a manufacturing district like Batley.

Batley Football Club may have been both the leading and most successful club in the town, but it was not the only rugby football club in Batley. The *Hull Daily Mail*, 28th August 1890, in listing details of the "Yorkshire Challenge Cup Draw" for 1891, reveals the existence of Batley Mountaineers and Batley Gipsies, either of which could have been drawn against Batley in the second stage of the competition. It may be that the success of Batley's premier club acted as an inspiration to their less well-known neighbours.

Bumps in the road

In spite of the success and ambition of the club, the 1890s was not without its challenges, both for the club as a whole and some individual players. Perhaps the most significant, particularly with regard to the club's long term future, was the task of ensuring financial stability. This was not a problem that was unique to Batley Football Club, but it was a problem that continued to dog the club throughout the 20th century, and one which necessitated a whole range of fund raising activities. The *Yorkshire Evening Post*, 8th November 1894, reported that:

The Batley Cricket, Athletic and Football Club is in the unhappy position of having an adverse balance at the bank of between four hundred and five hundred pounds, and special efforts are to be made to reduce the deficit, or if possible to wipe it out. The Committee have passed a resolution to hold a bazaar next Easter.... The club's debt is felt to be a heavy drawback to the club, and subscriptions, and cricket and football receipts are insufficient to cover expenses and decrease the sum owed to the bank.

The bazaar was actually held in February 1895 as a result of concerns that Easter would not be the most propitious time for such an event. The following year both the *Yorkshire Evening Post*, 21st February 1896, and the *Leeds Mercury*, 24th February 1896, carried reports about a three day bazaar which had been held in aid of Batley C.A. and F.C. The *Leeds Mercury* noted that "This bazaar, which was opened last Thursday, closed on Saturday evening. Six hundred pound was required, and the receipts are only a few pounds below."

However, the *Yorkshire Evening Post* sounded a more ominous note:

There is a likelihood of the Mount Pleasant enclosure being taken out of the hands of the club and laid out for building sites, and the idea prevails that the club should buy the field... It is stated that a sum of between two thousand and three thousand pounds would cover the cost, and that if the present chance be lost the club would have the greatest difficulty in finding suitable quarters elsewhere.

The idea that the club should purchase the ground was a very sensible one and, as will be seen subsequently, that is exactly what Batley C.A. and F.C did in 1898, thereby securing its long term future at Mount Pleasant.

By far the most sensational issue that the 'Gallant Youths' had to deal with in the early 1890s was the accusation, in 1892, that Herbert Simms and Tom Elliker had "sold" (taken a bribe to lose) a Yorkshire Challenge Cup match against Heckmondwike (played at Bramley). This was an extremely serious accusation which, if proven, could have led to dire consequences both for the individuals concerned and the club as a whole. The integrity of those who were accused was rigorously defended by the club's trainer, Richard Webster (London Dick), and various members of the Batley Football Club Committee. The *Yorkshire Evening Post*, 28th April 1892, covering the matter in some detail, reported that Richard Webster

....had seen one of the players who was accused and this person (Herbert Simms) was prepared at any moment to come before the committee and explain all he knew.

The newspaper, adding that Webster believed that the Batley

Committee should do all in its power to clear Simms' name, went on to outline Mr. W. Brearley's stout defence of Tom Elliker:

Mr. W. Brearley, on behalf of Elliker – one of the players whom rumours accused of treacherous conduct – offered to give five pounds to any man who could prove that Elliker had either sold the match at Bramley, or received any benefit from losing in any way shape or form, whatever, against one pound laid down by the party lodging a complaint and proving it.

In the end the matter was dropped and no action was taken against either of the accused. At this distance from the events it is impossible to know whether there was any truth at all in the accusations that were levelled against Elliker and Simms. It is true that the team's performance in the game against Heckmondwike was, by all accounts, a poor one, but it may be that this was simply a consequence of Batley being forced to replay a game which they believed they had legitimately won. Heckmondwike's objection to Batley's winning try in the initial fixture had been upheld by the County Committee, which then ruled that the game must be replayed. In fairness, it should also be pointed out that, as we shall see, neither Tom Elliker nor "Dodger" Simms were uncomplicated individuals, though this does not mean that they would have been prepared to accept a bribe to "throw" a game. It might also be doubted whether two individuals from a team of fifteen could have ensured that a game was lost without drawing undue attention to themselves during the course of the match. No claim was made that either player had deliberately gifted points to the opposition or wilfully failed to score.

Financial difficulties and accusations of bribery were not the only "bumps in the road" that Batley Football Club encountered during the 1890s. The "extra-curricular" activities of some of the players occasionally caused embarrassment for the club. In 1891, 1892 and 1893 the *Yorkshire Evening Post* contained stories about members of the Batley team who had appeared in court. The edition on the 21st December 1891 included the following article under the heading "A Batley Football Player Fined":

At West Riding Police Court, Dewsbury, today, Mark Shackleton, one of the forwards of Batley Football team, was fined 7s. 6d. and costs for using obscene language in Station Lane, Soothill, on the night of the 12th. The evidence of Mr. John Grimshaw, the instructor of the Batley Volunteers, was that he was going down the lane in the company of his wife when Shackleton insulted them. Defendant was the worse for liquor at the time, and had since apologised. Shackleton made no reply to the charge.

On 6th December 1892, the *Yorkshire Evening Post* featured a story under the heading "A Batley Football Player's Failure – His Business Ruined by Bad Beer":

Today at Dewsbury Bankruptcy Court, Herbert Simms, a prominent player in the Batley team, and who has several times done duty for his county, was examined at some length by Mr. E.E. Deane, the Official Receiver, in regard to his affairs. He (Mr. Simms) said that after being in the waste trade he took the Bull and Butcher Inn, Batley, and remained there for three years. The house was tied and he was supplied with bad beer.

He had no account of his takings, but he believed they would amount to fifteen pounds. He received a month's notice to quit after being prosecuted. The second prosecution was for alleged betting on his premises and he was convicted.

Towards the Schism

Ten months later, the same newspaper reported the following:

Yesterday at Dewsbury's County Court, Edwin Jackson, a prominent player of the Batley Football Club, and who has done duty several times for his county, was examined in respect of his affairs. He said he became landlord of the Cross Keys Inn, Morley, in February 1889. He did very well for the first twelve months, but then there was a strike among the quarrymen, and he could get rid of plenty of ale, but could not get paid for it.

Perhaps stories about rugby players behaving inappropriately whilst under the influence of alcohol or demonstrating a lack of business acumen are hardly surprising, but they certainly generated unwelcome publicity for the club. Of course, such falls from grace by individual players may not have damaged team morale, but local and regional newspapers, in the hope of boosting their circulation, were constantly on the lookout for stories that would excite the interest of the fans, sometimes without regard to the impact it may have on the team. Consequently, the *Yorkshire Evening Post*, 28th February 1893, contained the following report under the heading "Rumoured Resignation of James Naylor":

A rumour was circulating in Batley yesterday to the effect that Jimmy Naylor, the popular half-back, had sent in his resignation as a member of the Batley Football Club, in consequence of his dissatisfaction at the neglect of selected players to turn up in ordinary matches away from home.

This rumour was, to some extent, echoed in the 1960s and 70s with regard to the so-called "Hull Flu Syndrome", in connection with which it was claimed that some players who did not look forward to a tough game at The Boulevard would fall victim to a mystery virus in the run up to the game. We cannot, of course, discount the fact that in 1893 the main cause of this problem may have been the issue of "broken time". Travelling to away matches was time consuming and may, for some players, have resulted in a considerable loss of earnings.

The same newspaper, on 23rd June 1893, featured another story about a well-known Batley player:

Considerable comment is being raised in Batley by the sudden disappearance of Tom Elliker, the popular half-back of the Batley Football Club. Elliker, who kept the Prince of Wales Inn, in Cobden Street, left home last Monday without saying anything as to where he was going, and up to this morning has not been heard of.

Elliker, who was coming to the end of his career, and whose disappearance was never explained, turned out for Pudsey, a village club, in a game against Buttershaw on Saturday 16th September 1893, though he did return to play some games for Batley, most notably during the first season under the auspices of the Northern Union.

Arguably, the most acute problem that the club faced in the early 1890s was one over which it had limited control: small pox. In 1892 there was an outbreak of smallpox in the town, and in an era prior to the introduction of mass vaccination the spread of this devastating disease was difficult to control. Potentially, Batley could have been unable to play any home games whilst the epidemic was in full spate. In the event the worst effects, as far as the club's fortunes were concerned, were avoided, though not without considerable effort on the part of the Batley Football Club

Committee. According to the *Yorkshire Evening Post*, 18th March 1892 and *Batley News*, 25th March 1892, Goole were very reluctant to play their Yorkshire Challenge Cup match against Batley at Mount Pleasant on 19th March 1892, preferring to have the fixture relocated to either Goole or a neutral ground. This suggestion was unacceptable to the Batley Football Club Committee, which, as reported in the *Y.E.P*, produced the following certificate and additional note signed by the Borough Sanitary Officer, Mr. Joseph Lindley:

Sir, - Smallpox has certainly been prevalent in Batley, but it is now almost extinguished. Further, the Isolation Hospital is two miles out of town, and in the extreme opposite part to the cricket and football field.

I also am glad to state that any person may now visit Batley without any danger of contracting smallpox.

The match, which Batley won, took place as scheduled, but as the Batley correspondent of the *Y.E.P* pointed out on 27th April 1890, neither the town nor the club had emerged from the epidemic unscathed:

Shopkeepers of Batley have been detrimentally affected by people staying away....The Batley Football Club too have been made to suffer in this matter.

The Schism

The story of the formation of the Northern Union in 1895 has been told elsewhere, most notably in Tony Collins's magnificent *Rugby's Great Split* (1998, Frank Cass), but it is worth taking some time to examine the context in which clubs such as Batley took the momentous decision to break away from the National Rugby Union. The decision to form the Northern Union did not come out of the blue, as the potential fault line within the National Rugby Union had been visible several years earlier. In 1886 Batley's refusal to re-play their Yorkshire Challenge Cup semi-final against Halifax on Wednesday 7th April was underpinned by the issue of "broken time". Batley forfeited the trophy they had won the previous year rather than play, unnecessarily as they saw it, another mid-week match which would cause the players to lose money by taking time off work. The decision to schedule the re-play on Wednesday had been taken by the County Committee of the Yorkshire Rugby Union, so it was, perhaps, no surprise that the *Yorkshire Post*, 26th November 1891, reported that:

On Tuesday evening a meeting of the representatives of the clubs comprising of the Batley district of the Yorkshire Football Union was held at the Royal Hotel, Batley, for the purpose of forming a Rugby Union for the district.

The article also referred to district Unions in Castleford and Bradford, so it seems clear that amongst some of the clubs in Yorkshire, those in industrial areas, there was a desire for more autonomy. The Yorkshire County Committee began to take notice of the concerns that were being expressed at a local level within the county, as was recorded in an article in the *Yorkshire Evening Post*, 28th February 1893, which highlighted the fact that the County Committee was giving serious consideration to a "suggestion that competitions should be arranged for the clubs in certain districts which may be grouped together for this purpose...." This suggestion was designed to reduce the amount of travelling time required for away matches, time which might impinge on working hours and thus result in a loss of earnings. By 1893 the issue of "broken time", which was clearly creating divisions within the sport, was being openly discussed in the press. The *Yorkshire Evening Post*, 18th September 1893 noted that:

Just now everybody who takes the slightest interest in football is talking about "broken time". To pay or not to pay, that is the question, and it will be settled – and Yorkshiremen think satisfactorily settled – at the annual meeting of the English Rugby Union on Wednesday evening. Yorkshire have decided to propose that players shall be recouped for the loss of time through taking part in matches; Mr. Cail, the President, and Mr. Rowland Hill, the hon. Secretary of the Union, as representing the official view of the subject, will endeavour to obtain a declaration from the meeting that such a payment is illegal.

Northern opinion, backed by Northern votes, does not that way tend. Here in Yorkshire, where the game is played by hundreds of working men, people do not take the aristocratic view of the winter pastime which seems to find so much favour in the South.

The nature of the division was now becoming clear, with class differences coming to the fore. Towards the end of 1894 the crisis escalated as clubs began to be suspended for contravening the Rugby Football Union's rules against professionalism. The *London Daily News*, which was singularly unsympathetic towards any clubs in breach of the rules, carried articles about the suspensions in its edition on 3rd and 10th November 1894. In the former edition, it was reported that:

The Rugby Union Committee sat for five hours in London discussing the matter and showed there were no half-measures dealing with it. Infringements of the rules will be met with expulsion from the Union – and clubs will have to prove their innocence when charged with professionalism.

At the same time there was an acknowledgement in the article that the problem, as the newspaper saw it, would not be easily resolved:

It is evident that the Union will not legalise professionalism, but the stamping out of the evil is likely to be difficult.

At this point it is worth examining the socio-political context in which this conflict took place. The Northern Union was formed in the wake of what many members of the aristocracy and landed gentry viewed as a century of creeping democracy. Parliamentary reform acts in 1832, 1867 and 1884 had extended the franchise, so that by the end of the 19th century approximately sixty percent of all adult males were eligible to vote. The Rugby Union's implacable opposition to the payment of rugby players might be seen as attempt, by those who considered themselves to be British society's traditional rulers, to consolidate their power and limit the power of the emerging working class. After all, those adult males who by 1895 were still not eligible to vote had frequently, in the recent past, been referred to as the "residuum", the leftovers who, almost by definition, were not worthy of consideration. The nature of the language used by those who opposed the Northern Union, which was officially established on 29th August 1895, is extremely revealing about their mindset and attitudes. Some of it is quasi-religious, using words such as heresy, schism and excommunication, whilst it is frequently suffused with a sickening paternalism which betrays an underlying contempt for those who have had the temerity to challenge the established authority. The aforementioned article from the *London Daily News*, 3rd November 1894, referred to professionalism as "the evil", whilst the words of Mr. G. Rowland Hill in his address to the Rugby Union Committee, as reported in the *Yorkshire Post*, 20th September 1895, are worth quoting at length as a prime example of the paternalistic attitude referred to above:

Long years ago when I had the honour of being the Secretary of your Union, at a time when football was comparatively little played except those clubs coming more from our public schools. I, year after year, visited nearly every part of Great Britain, watching our game, and I saw gradually coming up a new class – the working class – taking a deep interest in our game. As one who has always held some good old-fashioned Tory notions, in good friendship to the working classes, I looked with a passionate delight on this development. But unfortunately dangers have come. Those who ought to have led the working men properly have, I deeply regret to say, led them astray.

It is for that class that I feel so keenly sorry today- these men who but for a few years will be able to take payment for broken time or for anything else. It will only last a little time. Then, when they have been encouraged to neglect their legitimate occupation, those who ought to know better will not help them to get other employment. That, I am perfectly convinced of.

....I do hope that those who have real social influence among the working classes will use it if they can to point out the evils which I am perfectly convinced are before them.

At best, it might be argued that Mr. Hill, from his own perspective, was attempting to save working class men from their own folly, but perhaps the most instructive words in the above passage are those which refer to "our game". Mr. Rowland Hill's proprietorial approach to Rugby Football suggests that the interests of the sport are synonymous with the interests of his social class.

The *Western Daily Press*, Bristol, 20th September 1895, whilst broadly sympathetic to the Rugby Football Union, recognised the potential threat posed by the "secessionist" Northern Union, particularly given that the latter was considering rule changes which this newspaper acknowledged might result in the game becoming more open and therefore more pleasurable and exciting for the spectators. However, the Rugby Football Union, unable to bring the northern schismatics to heel, set out to isolate the Northern Union, adopting a strategy that was to continue well into the 20th century. The *Huddersfield Daily Chronicle*, 7th September 1895, under the heading "The Rugby Union and the Northern Union" reported that:

The following communication has been received from Mr. G. Rowland Hill, hon. Secretary of the Rugby Football Union :- "In answer to an enquiry from one of our clubs asking if they would be permitted to play matches at present arranged with clubs which have joined the Northern Union, I have replied as follows:- I am directed by my committee to inform you that no club belonging to our Union will be permitted to play matches with any club which is in membership with the Northern Union.

This policy of no contact was pursued to extreme, and often farcical, lengths, as a story from the *Hull Daily Mail*, 25th January 1898 serves to illustrate:

Considerable resentment is being felt by the members of the Goole Football Club at the action of the Yorkshire Rugby Union in reference to a proposed Charity Match which was to take place at Goole on Thursday. The match proposed was one between a

Towards the Schism

Pantomime Company and the local football team. Before definitely deciding upon the fixture, the Secretary of the Goole club wrote to the Rugby Union for permission to play the match, at the same time mentioning that the same company played Batley, a Northern Union team, a short time ago. The Secretary has now received a reply to the effect that the Union have decided not to allow the match to be played.

Clearly, the mistake that the Goole Secretary made was to mention that their prospective opponents had played against a Northern Union club, albeit in a charity match. The involvement of a pantomime company in this incident serves well as a metaphor for the subsequent behaviour of the Rugby Football Union towards the Rugby Football League, other than that pantomimes can be amusing whereas the behaviour of the Rugby Football Union was simply vindictive.

The Glory Years

It was therefore in the context of the debate about "broken time" payments and professionalism that Batley opted to be part of the Northern Union from the date of its inception in August 1895. Batley's first match under the auspices of the Northern Union was played against Hull at Mount Pleasant on 7th September 1895. Batley won the game by seven points to three, from a try scored by Spurr and a drop goal by Shaw. In the absence of an authentic official teamsheet, there is a degree of uncertainty about the composition of the Batley team for this first match, but the following is as accurate as it can be at the moment: Lane, I. Shaw, J. Goodall, Joe Naylor, J. Oakland, Jim Naylor, T. Elliker, M. Shackleton, Paudie Munns, F. Fisher, J. Littlewood, C. Stubley, R. Spurr, T. Wilby, J. Welsh

It is possible that A. Garner played instead of Lane and that F. Bennett played instead of Welsh.

This first season was not a particularly successful season given that Batley lost twenty four of the forty two matches played, drew six and won only twelve. Consequently this was a somewhat inauspicious start to the new era, but at the commencement of the 1896-1897 season the club was determined to revive past glories, as outlined by the Batley correspondent in the *Yorkshire Evening Post*, 31st August 1896, who wrote that:

A determined attempt is to be made this year to once more bring about the former prestige of the club. It is believed there is enough talent to do this. Every opportunity is now being taken by the first team to develop good form, and practice takes place on the Mount Pleasant ground two or three times a week.

Over the next two years not only was this goal achieved, but it was superseded, as Batley's legendary status as the inaugural winners of the Rugby League Challenge Cup was established. However, in December 1896 Batley Football Club was in the news for an entirely different reason, one which recurs on several subsequent occasions. Apparently, at the end of the match between Batley and Brighouse Rangers, on Saturday 19th December, a game which Brighouse did not want to play because of the state of the pitch, a major fracas took place, occasioned, it seems, by some foul play on the part of the Brighouse team after the final whistle had been sounded. Needless to say, the Brighouse players denied that one of their number had punched Wattie Davies in the mouth after the whistle had sounded. The *Yorkshire Evening Post* covered the whole incident in detail across two editions on 22nd and 23rd December 1896. The latter edition contained a letter from a Brighouse supporter who, having attended the match, wrote to the newspaper to express his dismay at the general behaviour of the Batley supporters. The following is a brief extract from the letter:

Another instance of a sample of the Batley spectators' temper was displayed on the stand, through an incident which took place during the second portion of the game, when one of the home supporters threatened to pitch a Brighouse visitor from top to bottom of the stand, for simply expressing an opinion on the game.

In the interests of balance, of course, the same newspaper included a detailed commentary on the events by the *Y.E.P.*'s Batley correspondent who concluded his piece with the observation that: "....the Batley Committee are quite prepared – indeed anxious – to meet any charges that may be brought in reference either to the state of the ground on Saturday or to the charge of "rough and brutal treatment by the Batley spectators."

In the end, nothing came of this dispute, leaving Batley free to concentrate on preparing for the Northern Union Challenge Cup competition which was due to commence in early Spring 1897. Batley progressed to the quarter finals, having beaten Bramley and Brighouse Rangers on the way, where they were drawn at home against Widnes, whom they defeated, after which the *Eastern Morning News*, 12th April 1897, reporting that Batley, Warrington, Swinton and St. Helens had reached the semi-finals, also noted that: "Despite the fact that the odds are 3 to 1 against the trophy coming to Yorkshire, Batley are playing so well that the chances of their winning are far from remote." Batley dispatched Warrington in the semi-final, which was held at Fartown, and faced St. Helens in the final at Headingley on Saturday, 24th April

1897. On that day, the *Lancashire Daily Post*, which might have been expected to favour St. Helens, noted that: "The Cup Competition has proved decidedly interesting, and the probable winners of the pot are Batley." This prediction was accurate, and though the St. Helens team may have been hampered by the fact that the team's kit was stolen before the game, the general consensus was that Batley were worthy victors. The final score was Batley ten points against three for St.Helens. The *People*, 2nd May 1897, emphasized Batley's superiority over their opponents: "The game was keenly contested, but that Batley thoroughly deserved to win no one will deny who witnessed the struggle, for they had by far the best of matters throughout."

As indicated by the above extract, the inaugural final was widely reported on. In addition to the report in the *Batley News*, as might be expected, one of the most detailed reports of the match appeared in the *Liverpool Mercury*, 26th April 1897, from which the following extracts convey a sense of the enthusiasm and excitement which prevailed amongst both fans and players on this momentous day:

The enormous interest which centred in the final-tie on Saturday was evidenced by the crowded excursion trains which poured into Leeds from St. Helens, Manchester, Batley, and other Yorkshire towns, and the splendid enclosure at Headingley, which is estimated to hold 25,000 people, was packed long before the time announced for the kick off. All the leading lights of the Northern Union occupied reserved seats on the grand stand, and as the teams entered the arena great enthusiasm prevailed. The St. Helens men were the first to appear, and were cordially greeted, but the Batley team had a perfect ovation.

....Oakland picked up from a scrimmage and dropped a goal, five minutes from the start, amid the demonstrative enthusiasm of

the Yorkshire contingent of the spectators. This reverse spurred on the Lancastrians, who for a period confined operations to the Batley half, but the Yorkshiremen, with a strong rush, dribbled to the opposite end, where, after some scrambling play by the St. Helens defenders, Davies passed the ball to Goodall, who scored a try for Batley, to the great delight of their supporters.

The Batley team that day was: A. Garner, W. P. Davies, D. Fitzgerald, J. B. Goodall, I. Shaw, J. Oakland, H. Goodall, M. Shackleton, J. Gath, G. Maine, R. Spurr, F. Fisher, C. Stubley, J. Littlewood, J. T. Munns.

The celebrations which took place when the team returned to Batley with the trophy, on the evening after the final, matched and exceeded the celebrations following the victory in the Yorkshire Challenge Cup Final more than a decade earlier. As previously, the team was met with a fanfare of noise when the train arrived at the station, its arrival heralded by the detonation of one hundred fog signals, and as to the crowds which gathered to greet the conquering heroes, the *Yorkshire Evening Post*, 26th April 1897, made this observation:

To say that the thoroughfares – Station Road, Bradford Road, and Commercial Street – were almost blocked completely and further, that the Batley players were enthusiastically greeted by at least 30,000 spectators – equal to the entire population of the town – is not at all inside the mark.

....From the windows of hotels, shops, warehouses, and everyday residences people caught up the enthusiasm from below, and for more than an hour the passage of the victorious team through the streets was one "triumphal march". Flags and banners, and the colours of the Batley club, floated everywhere.

This victory was a massive achievement for the club, and one which put the town of Batley firmly on the map, but the club did not intend to rest on its laurels, as may be seen from the report in the *Leeds Mercury*, 2nd September 1897, about a celebratory dinner that was held at the Station Hotel, Batley the previous evening:

Mr. D. F. Burnley, President of the club,....congratulated the team on the honour they had brought to the club and to the town, and, although it had been said they would most probably never accomplish the feat again, he held that what they had done once they could do again if they only kept together

....Mr. Shaw (Secretary), in a few remarks, said they wished to show people that winning the cup last year was no flash in the pan and no fluke.

These remarks were very prescient, because that is exactly what Batley did: they retained the Cup in 1898. The start of the new season was accompanied by a change in the rules, introduced by the Northern Union, the most important result of which was the replacement of the line-out with a kick-out and a change in the value of points awarded for tries, goals and drop goals. This was the start of a process by which the Northern Union, and subsequently the Rugby Football League, sought both to differentiate itself from the Rugby Union and make the game quicker and more exciting. In order to reach the semi-final of the Challenge Cup, in which Batley defeated Salford by five points to nil, they had to beat St. Helens, Walkden, Castleford and Oldham in the previous rounds. The semi-final was played at Oldham on Saturday, 9th April 1898, and whilst both the *Yorkshire Evening Post*, 9th April 1898 and *Sheffield Daily Telegraph*, 11th April 1898, agreed that the Batley fans were outnumbered by those from

Salford, from where thirteen special trains had departed, the *Yorkshire Evening Post* noted that:

....the Oldham people favoured the chances of Batley, and many of them were seen displaying the colours of the Mount Pleasant men. This was largely owing to the bad reputation the Salford men made for themselves in the Salford v. Oldham contest. On the Watersheddings folk openly declared their hope that Batley would be victorious.

The *Hull Daily Mail*, 11th April 1898, in reporting on the semi-final victories for Batley and Bradford, claimed that the latter's convincing victory over Widnes by thirteen points to nil was likely to cause some trepidation amongst their opponents in the final. On paper, according to the *Hull Daily Mail*, Bradford were the favourites, but the newspaper expected Batley to prevail: "In Senior Competition matches the two clubs have met twice this season, the first game being drawn and the second won by Bradford. This record should lead us to look to Bradford to supply the winners, but I have faith in Batley's cup-tie prowess, and therefore expect them to retain the Cup."

Bradford, it seems, did have a formidable record during the 1897-1898 season, having remained undefeated in twenty five consecutive matches before they faced Batley at Headingley on 23rd April, 1898, and were seeking to achieve the "double" by winning both the Championship and the Challenge Cup. The *Yorkshire Evening Post*, 18th April 1898 reported that: "....their supporters are confident that they will be able to pull off the 'double event'." Thus Batley, in spite of the fact that they were the current cup holders, arrived at the final as the underdogs. The Batley team that day was the same as the one which had contested the final the previous year, save for Fozzard on the wing instead of Shaw and Rodgers in the pack instead of Littlewood. The previous week, 'Old Ebor' in the *Yorkshire Evening Post*, 16th April 1898, had observed that:

....there are few teams in the Northern Union who have less imported players than Batley. Eleven out of the Cup fifteen are bona-fide Batley men and received their early football training in the town. Of the other four, Garner and Fisher are from the Huddersfield district, though they have both worked in Batley for five years, and were practically brought out by the Batley club. The two Welshmen, Fitzgerald and Davies, are really the only "foreigners" in the team.

The *Batley News*, 22nd April 1898, as part of the build up to the game, drew a contrast between the preparations for the final undertaken by the two teams, a contrast which reinforced the image of Batley as the underdogs:

When we enquired as to how Batley were training, we were told that they were doing a bit after 6 o'clock in the evening. However, from other, and evidently more reliable sources, we found that last Sunday week the players and committee had a pleasant trip to Morecambe, and all were much better for the outing. The players have been taking care of themselves all week.... At six o'clock every evening , there has been a full muster of the players on the ground, and after an hour's spin, a general adjournment has followed to the headquarters – The County Restaurant, where a capital spread has been set before them.

On the other hand, the Batleyites, with the exception of about three who are at present out of a "gif", have all been working during the week, not a few of them in the coal mine.

Towards the Schism

The same edition of the newspaper, which had extensive coverage of the upcoming final, included pen portraits of all the members of the Batley team, so we know that Fozzard, aged thirty three, was the oldest member of the team, in addition to the fact that, though he was referred to as "Fred", his actual name was Ted. The replacement for Littlewood, Jack Rodgers, aged twenty, was the youngest member of the team, having in the words of the *Batley News*, "sprung to prominence very quickly."

As to the event itself, the *Yorkshire Evening Post*, 23rd April 1898, provided a very detailed account of the scene at Headingley. It seems that the railway companies had gone out of their way to accommodate the large numbers of spectators that were expected to travel to the match by train, whilst at the same time seeking to avoid disruption to their normal Saturday afternoon services. Consequently, the "special" trains arrived at Kirkstall or Headingley, in an attempt to avoid very large numbers converging at the central station. The newspaper painted a very dramatic picture of the way in which the stadium became filled to capacity:

It was approaching half past 2 o'clock when people might be said to have begun to literally pour into the field. At that time there would be perhaps 6,000 to 7,000 present. From every converging point they could be seen surging in palpitating masses to the various entrances. Then, as if by magic, a sea of faces settled round the arena. Three o' clock arrived, and it looked utterly impossible for another spectator to find room in the gigantic multitude. But still the entrances were besieged by clamourous crowds.

As for the game itself, it was, by all accounts a very exciting contest, but one which Batley were never in danger of losing.

The key to Batley's victory, by seven points to nil, seems to have been the performance of the pack, which dominated their opponents, along with a carefully organised system of defence. The *Hull Daily Mail*, 25th April 1898, under the heading "Batley Win 'Hands Down' ", had this to say about the match and the performance of the Batley team:

Never did the excitement flag, but it was intensified in the second half .... Bradford's forwards were hopelessly thrashed, and it was to their own front rank mainly that Batley owe their victory. Upon the comparatively few occasions Bradford did get the ball, their backs were swamped before they had any chance to use it. Indeed, Batley's clever "spotting" was one of the features in a splendid game, and I never remember seeing a team practise this style with so much success as did the winners on Saturday.

The triumphant team returned home once again to large cheering crowds, though the *Batley News*, 29th April 1898, thought that "the excitement did not reach such a pitch as last year; it appeared rather a "welcome home again." Nonetheless, according to the newspaper "the streets were packed with thousands of folk, and the voices of young and old mingled in noisy wishes of success to the 'gallant youths'." The importance of this second successive victory in the Challenge Cup Final, both for the club and the town, can scarcely be exaggerated. This was a record that could not be erased, and one which would always be referred to in any consideration of the origins of the Rugby League Challenge Cup. For a relatively small town such as Batley, the prestige accrued from these successive triumphs was incalculable. At a complimentary dinner held for the team and the club officials at the Station Hotel on Wednesday 27th April 1898, Councillor Mr. J. Law, as recorded in the above edition of the

Towards the Schism

Batley News, outlined one of the key benefits the town derived from its rugby football team. Apparently, he had claimed that:

As a town Batley were indebted to football, because in a community like their own, where a large proportion of the population were engaged in mills and factories, it was most essential that they should be able to spend their time in the open air, and in order to encourage them to do that it was necessary to have something to entertain them. In the football season they had a team whom anyone could spend an hour and a half or two hours agreeably in witnessing them play.

Immediately prior to the start of the 1898-1899 season the local newspapers reported that the recently-elected captain of the team, Jim Gath, wished to be granted a transfer to Bradford, but that his request had been turned down by the Batley Football Club Committee. The *Reporter*, 19th August 1898 was sure that Bradford had set out to lure Gath with the promise of more money. Gath himself, whilst acknowledging that he wanted to play for Bradford, took exception to the claims that he had been directly approached by that club. He wrote a lengthy letter, which was printed in the *Reporter*, 26th August 1898, in which he set out his position:

....I am anxious and willing to play for Bradford, if the Batley club will give me my transfer – and bear in mind, and I hope the public will not forget this point, that I have never once been approached on the subject by any officials of the Bradford club....

I have been told that in the other Batley journal a suggestion has been made that I have been offered a situation in Bradford at 10s per week. Well, all I can say is that the cheek and impudence of some people seems boundless. It's nothing more or less than rank tom-foolery to say or think such a thing, and the man who wrote it should have known better.

This extract, unless the letter had been heavily edited, reveals that Jim Gath, in addition to being an outstanding player, was also a very literate individual. In the end he did not transfer to Bradford, but continued to turn out for Batley for the next couple of seasons. In October 1898, almost certainly on the back of successive victories in the Challenge Cup Final, the Batley Football Club Committee outlined a plan to purchase the ground for the sum of £2,300 (£289,903 equivalent in 2018) and aimed to raise £1500 by subscription. The purchase of the ground was important for an ambitious club, because it would give the club committee control of the estate. In the event, as we shall see, the purchase was not completed until 1904, since the wheels tend to grind slowly with regard to these matters. Unfortunately, 1898 ended on a sour note for Batley with the suspension of Dai Fitzgerald for a breach of the Northern Union's employment regulations which stipulated the types of additional employment in which those deemed to be full professionals could engage. There is some evidence to suggest that, in order to enforce this rule, the Northern Union was prepared to resort to extreme measures, as outlined in the *Yorkshire Evening Post*, 3rd December 1898:

Questioned on how malpractices were discovered, our informant (a senior official in the Northern Union) said the Northern Union gave the sub-committee full powers to employ private detectives to follow a player to see what job he had. Thus no player knew when he was watched.... Club rivals, too, were always glad to give information of any suspicious case.

The club was fined £60, a substantial sum in 1898, but as the *Yorkshire Evening Post*, 20th January 1899, recorded, the people of Batley rallied round to help Batley Football Club pay the fine: "The public subscription started in Batley in connection with the recent fine of £60 imposed on the Batley Football Club now amounts to £75 odd."

In spite of the spectre of the fine hanging over the club, 1899 had begun on a more amusing, if not slightly bizarre note. The *Batley News*, 6th January 1899, in its "Latest Football Jottings" had the following story under the heading "Alleged Attempted Kidnapping":

On Tuesday night at a meeting of the Dewsbury Northern Union Club.... strong complaints were made by at least two members of the committee of alleged kidnapping on the part of certain players belonging to the Batley club.

It was stated that Cockin had been pressed to play with Batley since his performance against the crack club on the Mount Pleasure enclosure last week.

With regard to the allegation made against the Batley players, I can only say that the accused treat the matter as a joke .... Perhaps neither the Dewsbury Committee nor their players know that "the gallant youths" have a reputation for chaffing. My own idea is that Cockin has been one of their latest victims.

Other than the fact that Batley's thirteen match winning streak in the Challenge Cup came to an end against Leigh on 1st April 1899, the 1898-1899 season was an extremely successful one for the club. Winning twenty three of their thirty league fixtures, Batley finished, for the first time, as champions of the Yorkshire Senior Competition. Off the field, the club was also breaking new ground, as reported in the *Yorkshire Evening Post*, 4th March 1899:

The Committee of the Batley Cricket, Athletic and Football Club have now on hand a scheme for forming the organisation into a

Limited Liability Company, with a capital of £7,000. Full details are not yet available, but it may be mentioned that shares are to be offered to the public, and that alterations include the erection of a substantial stone wall round three sides of the cricket and football enclosure (one side being already provided for), the re-arranging of the football area and grandstands, and the erection of a large pavilion.

Thus Batley C.A. and F.C. was making ambitious plans as the 19th century drew to a close, though it would take several years for those plans to be realised. Some of the challenges which lay ahead in the new century could have been anticipated, whilst others, most particularly the impact that the First World War would have on the club, could not.

TIMELINE: 1900 – 1914
UK and World Events

1900 – The Boxer Rebellion takes place in China
The Conservative Party wins the 'khaki' general election
1901 – The death of Queen Victoria
Marconi sends the first radio signal across the Atlantic
1902 – The Second Boer War ends
Local Education Authorities are established under the Balfour Act
1903 – The Women's Social and Political Union (Suffragettes) is founded
Wright Brothers make first man-powered flight
1904 – Car number plates are introduced in the UK
The Entente Cordiale between Britain and France is agreed

Towards the Schism

1905 –   The Trans-Siberian Railway is completed
          The British Red Cross Society is inaugurated
1906 –   The San Francisco earthquake results in
          approximately 3,000 deaths
          The Trades Disputes Act legalises picketing in the
          UK
1907 –   The Old Bailey Criminal Court opens in London
          Florence Nightingale receives the Order of Merit
1908 –   The Model T Ford goes on sale in the USA
          Bisto gravy powder is introduced in the UK
1909 –   160 miners killed in the West Stanley Pit Disaster,
          Co. Durham
          Lloyd George introduces The People's Budget
1910 –   The death of King Edward VII
          Jack Johnson becomes first black heavyweight
          boxing Champion
1911 –   The Parliament Act restricts the powers of the
          House of Lords
          The Official Secrets Act comes into effect
1912 –   The *Titanic* sinks on her maiden voyage
          The British Board of Film Censors is set up
1913 –   Stainless steel is invented in Sheffield by Harry
          Brearley
          439 miners die in Senghenydd Colliery Disaster in
          Wales
1914 –   The First World War begins
          The Panama Canal is opened

4

FROM TRIUMPH TO TRAUMA, 1900–1914

By the turn of the century Batley had, through its performances since 1895, built a formidable reputation and was, in spite of indifferent performances over the Christmas period, still one of the favourites to win the Yorkshire Senior Competition. As the *Yorkshire Evening Post*, 1st January 1900, pointed out: "Thus the sports people (outside Batley) will welcome the recent failures of a team that must still be regarded as the finest all-round combination in Yorkshire." As the new century dawned, expectations were high, expectations that were soon to be satisfied by yet another victory in the Challenge Cup Final. However, this was soon followed by a relatively lean period for the club, concerning overall performances and the acquisition of trophies.

In other ways there was an inauspicious start to the new century with regard to the general history of Batley C.A and F.C. Within the space of three months in early 1900 two deaths shook the club, the first one being a particularly unpleasant affair, as reported in the *Yorkshire Evening Post*, 11th January 1900: "A shocking discovery was made this morning in a field adjoining the Mount Pleasant football field at Batley, a collier named Arthur Armitage, residing at 44, Industrial Terrace, Mount Pleasant, being found dead with his throat cut. A blood stained razor was found near the body."

This unfortunate individual who, it seems, had committed suicide aged 28, had, in spite of outward appearances, been badly affected by the death of his brother. Less than three months later the same newspaper, on 31st March 1900, reported the death, from blood poisoning, of Alfred Shackleton, the brother of Mark Shackleton and a member of the Committee of Batley C.A. and F.C. This death was all the more poignant as it seems that Alfred Shackleton's blood poisoning was the result of a fragment of glass being left in his hand from an occasion, three years earlier, when he had put his hand through some glass whilst saving a boy from being trampled on at Batley Railway Station. The occasion was the gathering of fans eager to greet the triumphant members of the Batley team as they returned from their victory in the 1897 Challenge Cup Final; a very sad irony indeed.

As outlined in the previous chapter, in the latter years of the 19th century Batley C. A. and F.C. had ambitious plans both to purchase the Mount Pleasant field and launch the club as a limited liability company. These ideas were still current in the early 1900s and the *Bradford Observer*, 4th January 1901, included an article concerning an offer to the club that was to have some very important long term consequences for the fans:

Alderman Joseph Auty, a well-known temperance worker in Batley who from time to time has offered various sums of money to the Batley Football and Cricket Club, on condition the sale of intoxicants was discontinued, has had an interview with a deputation of club officials, and it has been arranged that alcoholic drink shall never be offered for sale on the Mount Pleasant enclosure again. Mr. Auty, in consideration of this undertaking, gives £500 and guarantees to raise £500 more amongst his friends.

Unless the general body of the members of the club disapprove of the action taken, efforts will be made to raise sufficient money to buy the Mount Pleasant field and secure it as a recreation ground for all time.

The *Manchester Courier and Lancashire General Advertiser,* 19th January 1901, reported that this offer, which had the unanimous backing of the club committee, was accepted by the members of Batley C.A. and F.C. at a meeting in Batley Town Hall on Thursday, 17th January 1901. Apparently, the attempt to raise money to purchase the ground through the creation of a limited liability company had failed, an ambition not realised until 1922, so Alderman Auty's offer was the only realistic means of achieving this goal. The above newspaper reported that Mr. James Goodall, the Batley president, believed that "The club had nothing to lose, but everything to gain by accepting the offer and agreeing to the conditions." Acceptance of the offer certainly enabled Batley Football Club to purchase the ground, a transaction which, as reported in the *Bradford Daily Telegraph,* 27th August 1904, was completed a few years later when the Batley Co-operative Society eventually paid the £500 it had promised to donate to the Auty scheme. This was an important milestone in the club's history, but it also meant that until the 1980s, when the restriction was removed, it was not possible for spectators to buy an alcoholic drink on the club's estate. This must have resulted in a considerable loss of revenue for the club, because though the Miners' Welfare Club, where alcoholic drinks could be purchased, was adjacent to the ground, it was not owned by Batley C.A. and F.C. This situation was, for many years, a source of frustration and bemusement for fans of visiting teams, who struggled to understand why they could not buy a pint at the Mount Pleasant ground.

From Triumph to Trauma

Nonetheless, without doubt the Auty family, in keeping with the role of small scale industrialists and tradesmen in the history of rugby league, made a major contribution to the development of Batley C.A. and F. and not just in regard to the purchase of the ground. Wilf Auty, who maintained his amateur status whilst playing for Batley, scored a try in the 1901 Challenge Cup Final victory over Warrington, whilst his cousins, William and Herbert Auty, both made their debut for Batley on the same day in 1906. The *Leeds and Yorkshire Mercury*, 1st December 1906, reported that:

William and Herbert Auty have played football with Healy Albion, a local junior team, and they have represented the heart and soul of that side. Their services have been at the disposal of Batley for some time, and they get their chance today against St. Helens at Mount Pleasant. The brothers are sturdy little fellows, and their initial appearance in better-class football company will be watched with much interest.

A Third Challenge Cup Trophy

Returning to matters on the field of play, in the final weeks of the 1899-1900 season Batley were very serious contenders for the Yorkshire Senior Championship. It was a very tight contest between them and their main rivals, Bradford, who, having both won and lost more but drawn fewer games than Batley, eventually prevailed by two points. The *Yorkshire Post*, 5th March 1900, highlighted the tense nature of the situation: "The Senior Competition tournament is concluding in a way that ought to satisfy the most enthusiastic adherent of the system. The winner of the Shield and the holder of the Wooden Spoon will probably not be known until the last match." Such was the tension, in fact, that when a referee from outside Yorkshire was appointed to officiate in Batley's penultimate league fixture against Bradford, at Bradford, Batley objected. The objection was rejected by a sub-committee of the Yorkshire Senior Competition and the ensuing game was a 0-0 draw. Bradford's triumph in the Championship was doubtless sweet revenge for their defeat by Batley in the 1898 Challenge Cup Final, a game that many pundits had expected them to win.

A year later, however, with the disappointment of having been pipped for The Yorkshire Senior Championship behind them, Batley, for the third time in five years, reached the final of the Challenge Cup. Along the way they had beaten Huddersfield, St. Helens, Runcorn and Oldham to contest the final against Warrington at Headingley on 27th April 1901. The *Manchester Courier and Lancashire General Advertiser*, on the day of the match, set up the contest thus:

So much has been written on the prospects of the Batley and Warrington clubs, who meet at Leeds this afternoon in the fifth final for the Northern Union Cup, that very little remains to be said. Both teams are confident of success, and if the glorious weather of this week continues, almost a record crowd may be looked for. It may be interesting to recall that when the teams met in the combined competition in 1895-96, the first season of the Northern Union, Batley won at home by 4 points to nil, and were beaten at Warrington by 6 points to 4.

A closely fought game was therefore expected and though the match received much less coverage in the newspapers than the association football Final, played at Bolton, the crowd at Headingley was larger than the crowd at Bolton. The *Manchester Evening News*, 29th April 1901, waxed lyrical about the size and enthusiasm of the crowd which exceeded 30,000:

From Triumph to Trauma

There were over 25,000 people present at the start, and as one or two belated trains were only then arriving in Leeds from Warrington the interval found the turnstiles still moving briskly. It speaks much for the holding capacity of the ground that there was still ample room. Yet some excited visitors were not satisfied, and a score or two of them must needs clamber on the roof of the Grand Stand, from which, with their lives in their hands, they secured a capital bird's-eye sort of view.

This newspaper, as might be expected, betrayed a little bias towards the Lancashire club in its reporting of the match, but was still able to praise the impenetrable Batley defence, noting that in cup ties played during the past five seasons only four teams (St. Helens, York, Leigh and Leeds Parish Church) had managed to score tries against Batley. Warrington were unable to add their name to that list as Batley, fielding eleven of the players who had appeared in the 1898 final, defeated them by six points to nil. The *Athletic News*, 29th April 1901, another Manchester-based newspaper, contained a very detailed report of the match. Of course, in the days before radio and TV broadcasts, for those fans unable to attend the game, a finely detailed report of the action was important. This particular blow-by-blow account charted the way in which Batley, in spite of having Maine sent off in the second half, turned the screw on their opponents once they had gone ahead through tries from "Wattie" Davies and Wilf Auty. The following extract from the *Athletic News*, taken from its account of the second half, provides a flavour of the proceedings:

Frequent infringements of the scrimmage gave the defenders (Warrington) the opportunities to kick away, but the Batley men were too strong, and repeatedly returned to the attack. Gradually, however, Warrington worked their way to the centre, but they never seemed dangerous, and as the minutes flew and time drew near the hopes of the Lancastrians faded.

Whilst the *Athletic News* acknowledged that Batley were worthy winners of the final, its overall praise for the victors was somewhat grudging, perhaps betraying a regional bias against the pre-eminent Yorkshire club. In claiming that Batley had overcome teams which were far superior to them with regard to the style of play, in itself a subjective judgement, the *Athletic News* paid Batley a back-handed compliment: "Prevention is better than scoring may be the new reading of the proverb according to Batley, and the men who have shown such a subtle and commanding power in the overthrow of adversaries may be said to have studied all the tricks which football is liable to."

The idea that Batley's success was built on the back of a very strong and resolute defence resonates with modern approaches to the game. The Australian national team has built its unprecedented dominance of the international game on the principle of prevention. Prevent your opponents from scoring, so goes the thinking, and scoring opportunities will arise for your team. Thus it seems that the Batley team of the early 20th century was well ahead of its time with regard to on-the field strategy. Meanwhile, the *Bradford Observer*, 29th April 1901, perhaps betraying a natural bias in favour of a Yorkshire team, was unequivocal in its praise for Batley:

Batley carried off the Cup in due course on Saturday, and every one of the 30,000 spectators at Headingley must have been convinced of the genuineness of the victory. There is no exact parallel to Batley's success in the Northern Union Cup-Ties. Indeed we are strongly of the opinion that three Cups, out of a total of five attempts, is likely to stand as a record for many years to come, possibly until generations have passed away.

This prediction was extremely prescient, for it was not until the period 1959-1963 during which Wakefield Trinity won three Challenge Cup Finals in four years, that this record was superseded. What neither Wakefield Trinity nor any other team could do was supersede Batley's record of having won the first two Challenge Cup Finals

The Lean Years 1902 -1907

In contrast to the stunning successes in previous years, there was a relative decline, both in terms of the team's performance on the field and with regard to the club's finances, during the period 1902-1907. Clearly the two were connected; in the absence of trophies, attendance at games fell and the club had less money to spend. The decline in performance was the result of a combination of factors: important players leaving or retiring; new players arriving and needing time to gel with the rest of the team – in other words a team in flux; other teams improving, having learnt by observing Batley; rule changes to which Batley took some time to adapt. This particular period illustrates the precarious nature of rugby league with regard to a club's stature. If Batley could so quickly fall from grace, then the same could happen to any club. This has not changed in the modern era of Super League. We need only look at the fate of Bradford Bulls in recent years and the current struggles of the Leeds Rhinos in seeking to rebuild in the wake of the retirement of key players, to realise that success can be ephemeral and difficult to recreate.

For the start of the 1901-1902 season, the General

Committee of the Northern Union decided to create a Northern Football League, one which comprised of only fourteen clubs as opposed to twenty two under the previous arrangements, in an attempt both to boost attendances at matches and improve performance levels. The Batley Committee was not particularly enthusiastic about the scheme but as the *Yorkshire Evening Post*, 5th June 1901, pointed out, felt that it had no choice but to support the proposal:

The decision of the Northern Union Committee to acquiesce in the formation of the new League was no surprise to Batley. Still, no-one appears greatly enamoured by the new order, many enthusiasts believing there was no need for such a League to be formed. On the other hand, it was felt to be a case of the Batley club going "with the swim", or being left out in the cold. The former alternative, of course, was chosen, and it is no secret that even the club's managers and officials are not over sanguine as to the success of the new organisation.

Batley had good reason to be wary about the new arrangements because the new League turned out to be more competitive. During the 1901-1902 season Batley won only eight of their twenty six league fixtures, suffering heavy defeats at the hands of Oldham, Leigh and Swinton. Part of the problem was that the team, though it had performed very well in the recent past, was an ageing team with few new players brought in for this season. Only Tom Fitzgerald, Harry Clayton and Fred Wilford, amongst the new faces at the club, played a substantial number of games. Other players, some elevated from the reserve team, made occasional appearances. Of course, this illustrates the difficulty of getting the balance right in the process of rebuilding an ageing team. There is no magic formula as to the ideal blend of new and experienced, but ageing, players.

Nonetheless, given the right occasion, Batley could still attract a large crowd to its home games, particularly if the opposing team was an old rival. On 29th March 1902, in a fixture against Bradford, a record crowd attended the game at Mount Pleasant. The *Batley News*, 4th April 1902, recorded that:

At half past three there were over 17,000 spectators in the field, including a thousand or two who could not possibly hope to get a glimpse of the game. Even the spiked tops of the cricket field railings were utilised as seats by scores of daring youths, and others were content to sit on the cricket ground and learn the progress of events from their more fortunate friends.

Reserved seat ticket holders had to fight their way through the throng, or suffer themselves to be passed over the heads of the crowd, and the players themselves had equal difficulty in getting into the enclosure.

Batley defeated Bradford by fifteen points to ten and the attendance that day is the second highest in the history of the club, superseded only by the all-time record set in March 1925 in a game against Leeds. 1902 may have been the start of a relatively lean spell for the club, but, for the moment, the team had retained its pulling power. Moreover, in spite of Batley's poor record in league games during the 1901-1902 season, the team still had sufficient collective muscle memory to progress to the semi-final of the Challenge Cup where they met Salford, having disposed of Brighouse Rangers, Altrincham, Bradford and Castleford along the way. Unfortunately, Batley lost to Salford by eight points to nil, so the victory against Warrington in the 1901 Challenge Cup

Final is still the high water mark of Batley's achievements in that competition.

The following season, 1902-1903, the team was more successful with fifteen wins, sixteen losses and three draws from thirty four league matches. For teams visiting Mount Pleasant the task was not as daunting as it used to be, but Batley could still go toe-to-toe with the league's strongest teams. At the beginning of February 1903 Batley faced Oldham, one of the favourites for the Championship, at Mount Pleasant and in a performance that was redolent of past triumphs, Batley defeated their Lancashire opponents by two points to nil. By all accounts, Batley's defence squeezed the life out of their opponents, who were unable to find a way through. It wasn't pretty, but it was effective.

The game against Halifax at Mount Pleasant on the 14th March 1903, was kicked off by Sir Redvers Buller, a General who had, before his sacking, been Commander-in-Chief of British Forces in South Africa during the early part of the Second Boer War. Apparently, the General had been persuaded by the Mayor and the Town Clerk that attendance at the football match would add an important dimension to his visit to the town. The *Batley News*, 21st March 1903, which contained a lengthy article about the General's visit to the town, described the scene at Mount Pleasant thus:

The carriages entered the field by the members' entrance, which had been decorated with streamers and bore a motto welcoming the General. The party was then driven to the small grand stand, where the visitors alighted, and were greeted by Mr. J. Goodall (President of the club), Mr. D. F. Burnley, Mr. W. G. Isherwood and Mr. W. H. Shaw. They were then conducted to the enclosure, a portion of which had been reserved for them. Across the top were the words "Welcome to General Buller." As they took their seats a loud cheer went up from the huge crowd assembled, and Sir Redvers lifted his hat in acknowledgement. The cheer was redoubled when it was announced that Sir Redvers had consented to kick-off and it was renewed when Sir Redvers walked onto the field .... the ball was specially provided by a local firm, and inscribed on it were the words "The Mount of Valour", reminiscent of the place where Sir Redvers won his V.C.

This event was one of the highlights of the year as far as Batley C. A. and F.C was concerned because by the end of the season the outlook for the club was somewhat gloomy, particularly with regard to its finances. On 23rd May 1903, both The *Yorkshire Post* and the *Leeds and Yorkshire Mercury* reported that the club's debt had increased by £165 during the past financial year. The latter newspaper claimed that: "It is said that this deficit is accounted for by the Batley team's inability to maintain their reputation in the cup-ties."

Both newspapers highlighted the fact that the cumulative revenue from Batley's last four home matches only amounted to £60, some way short of the £200 such games normally realised. The price of failure in a competition which Batley had once dominated was high. The reports in both these newspapers betray a sense of surprise that Batley's finances had deteriorated so rapidly, but as mentioned earlier, this is a theme running through both the history of rugby league in general and Batley Rugby Football Club in particular. Even in the era of Super League and enhanced revenues from TV, major clubs have faced the threat of bankruptcy and in one case succumbed. By 1907 the club's finances had further deteriorated to the point where, as reported in the *Leeds and Yorkshire Mercury*, 22nd February 1907: "A few weeks ago the committee and players met and it was suggested that half-wages should be paid for the rest

of the season. Adopted on the suggestion of Wattie Davies –
reminding colleagues half a loaf better than none."

There was a suggestion in both the above newspaper
and the *Batley News*, 22nd February 1907, that, such were the
state of the club's finances, Batley C.A. and F.C. might have
to consider the formation of an association football team in
order to survive. "King Crow", in his column in the *Batley
News*, was unequivocal about what lay ahead:

*Whether we like it or not, we are bound to acknowledge that the
signs of the times unmistakably point to the probability –nay,
certainty- that the winter pastime of the future in Yorkshire will be
the game of Association football....*

*In fact broadly speaking, the handling code is not played at
all now by the youth of the Heavy Woollen District; it is all
Association.*

"King Crow's" suggestion was that an association football
team could run in tandem with the rugby team, playing at
Mount Pleasant when the latter was playing an away fixture.
He pointed out that, in the absence of a reserve team (in itself
a sign of financial constraints), the ground was underused. It
is likely that "King Crow" had been heavily influenced by the
creation of Bradford City Association Football Club in 1903,
which emerged from Manningham Football Club, and
possibly behind the scenes discussions that were taking place
at Bradford F.C. The latter, in what was subsequently known
as the "Great Betrayal", resulted in the replacement of rugby
at the Park Avenue ground by association football. In the
event, there was no equivalent betrayal at Mount Pleasant,
but, as the *Leeds and Yorkshire Mercury*'s report, 16th May 1907,
of the Batley C.A. and F.C.'s annual meeting demonstrated,
all was not well behind the scenes:

An unpleasant incident occurred on the appointment of the treasurer. Mr. H. Whitaker who had been treasurer for three years declined to hold the office again, – when Mr. Ellis Turner, junr. Said "Give him £5 and then he'll do it."

Mr. Whitaker strongly protested against this remark but Mr. Turner refused to withdraw it. Mr. Whitaker said it was an abominable insult. He added that in a public saleroom this week it had been said that the Committee had done better out of the club than the players.

Given that the club had, by this time, accrued a debt of £501, it is hardly surprising that there was tension amongst the members of the committee. However, leaving the club's finances aside for the moment, it is appropriate to return to the players and the team. At the start of the 1903-1904 season Batley recruited another Welshman by the name of Davies, W.T. Davies (Will), who served the club admirably for the next seven seasons. This new addition to the team was a source of confusion for the newspapers, many of which, as indicated earlier, struggled to record correct spellings of surnames. Both the *Leeds and Yorkshire Mercury*, 21st September 1903, and *Portsmouth Evening News*, 22nd September 1903, referred to Will Davies as "Wattie", which was, of course, the nickname of W. P. Davies. There is, perhaps, more excuse for the latter newspaper which was far removed from the industrial north, but the mistake further highlights the perennial problem associated with the the reporting of names, especially if newspapers are sharing copy.

The 1903-1904 season could not be described as a successful one. Out of thirty seven league and cup games played, Batley lost twenty, drew four and won only thirteen. More worryingly, the team failed to register a score at all on ten occasions. Of the players who made their debut's during the season, only Will Davies and Tom Phillips went on to make a substantial number of appearances before the season ended. Ted Fozzard, who had been a regular in the team since his debut in 1895, made thirty appearances. The club was undoubtedly in the doldrums and there seemed to be no immediate prospect of relief from this misery. Against this background of financial constraints and poor performances, the *Hull Daily Mail*, 13th February 1905, pulled no punches in its assessment of the competence of those who were running the club:

The Batley Management are chiefly to blame for the present precarious position. For several years they have seen the old players dropping out, one by one, and they have neglected to provide efficient reserves. Your "Watties", Oaklands, Goodalls and Shackletons cannot go on for ever and steps should have been taken to replace the old stand-backs.

The suggestion that the Batley committee had been complacent following the team's earlier successes is clearly visible below the surface of this article. Complacency precipitates a spiral of decline, as failure on the field results in reduced revenue at the turnstiles and reduced revenue inhibits the club's ability to recruit high quality players. This is not to say that managing the affairs of a rugby league club should be regarded as an easy task, but rather that those in charge need to be eternally vigilant with regard to a club's longer-term prospects. In February 1906, Batley stood in the bottom half of the league table and the *Leeds and Yorkshire Mercury*, 5th February 1906, in reporting on Batley's derby game against Dewsbury which had ended in a 0-0 draw, made what has, regarding Batley's current name, turned out to be a prophetic observation: "The game was not very old before it was seen that it was going to be a case of bull-dog defence and bull-dog attack. Each team was going to prevent the other from scoring at any cost, and gradually the players, encouraged by the spectators, began to introduce rough play."

Aside from the unintentionally prophetic bulldog reference, this brief extract attests to the very fierce rivalry between the two clubs. No two professional rugby league club grounds (at least in Britain) are closer to each other than those of Batley and Dewsbury, so the rivalry is all the more keenly felt. Indeed, the rivalry extends beyond the field of play and into the relations between the two towns at a civic level, which then feeds back into the sporting rivalry. This civic rivalry is no better illustrated than by an article in the *Yorkshire Evening Post*, 21st November 1905:

Batley folks (says a special correspondent of the Y.E.P) want nothing to do with Dewsbury's ambitious proposal to form a County Borough in the district....

The Batley authorities are sincerely sorry for their neighbours, but they fear that at present sympathy is the only thing they can offer them.

Apparently, Dewsbury's suggestion was that the County Borough should be formed from a combination of the Municipal Boroughs of Batley and Dewsbury plus the Urban District Council of Thornhill. This is probably a good example of local chauvinism and civic rivalry getting in the way of pragmatic judgement. It may very well have been in Batley's commercial interest to have been part of a County Borough, but this was not to be and Dewsbury went on to obtain County Borough status in 1913. The fear, perhaps, was that Batley's separate identity would be compromised once it was subsumed within a County Borough dominated by its rival. Also this might have had subsequent ramifications for the separate identity of its renowned Rugby Football Club, an identity that was to be protected at all costs.

In spite of Batley's indifferent performance 1905-06, during which season they lost eighteen of their thirty four league fixtures, the club's reputation endured amongst the rugby fraternity. The *Millom Gazette*, 2nd February 1906, reported that: "The game between Batley and Bramley was full of incident, and some of the home side's movements certainly reminded one of the time when the men of Mount Pleasant were at the top of the tree." The *Hull Daily Mail* and the *Leeds and Yorkshire Mercury*, 2nd April 1906, were both complimentary about Batley's performance in defeating Hull KR by fifteen points to nil in a cup-tie at Mount Pleasant. The former newspaper focused attention on what it considered to be the club's astute approach to the recruitment of new players:

In all conscience the result − Batley 15 points to the proverbial nil − is most unpleasant for the Rovers' officials to dwell upon, but I hope they will congratulate the Batley Management on their smart business-like qualities in the capture of clever players.

I was officially informed at Batley − and the veracity of the information cannot be doubted − that the largest amount paid by the Batley club to any player in securing his services is only £30, and that this sum was given to F. Loosemore, who plays centre to Wattie Davies. In White, the fullback, and Cookson, the half-back, both of whom were obtained from Castleford a few months ago, Batley possess two promising players. For their captures the Mount Pleasant club paid much less than £30.

The *Hull Daily Mail* correspondent gives no reason as to why the veracity of the information cannot be doubted, so it may be that he is simply parroting what he has been told by Batley Football Club, whose committee had good reason to promote a story that it was spending money wisely. Nonetheless, Batley supporters were, as the *Leeds and Yorkshire Mercury*, 2nd April 1906, put it "beginning seriously to indulge in visions of a Cup triumph, to add to their laurels of the past." Sadly, these visions were snuffed out in the next round of the Challenge Cup when Batley lost to Bradford by eleven points to three.

In the following season, 1906-1907, Batley appear to have been adversely affected by the Northern Union's decision to reduce the number of players in a team from fifteen to thirteen. In spite of the recruitment of a new half-back, "Mog" Bevan, from rugby union, the team won only seven of its twenty five league games, recording eleven consecutive losses in the league between 26th December 1906 and 1st April 1907. If that were not bad enough Batley suffered a heavy loss by thirty four points to nine against Warrington in the first round of the Challenge Cup. The *Athletic News*, 22nd October 1906, included a report of a fixture between Batley and Wakefield at Mount Pleasant, which Batley won by ten points to eight, under the heading "Farcical Football at Batley":

The game with Wakefield at Batley was characterised from end to end not by skilful movements and brilliant individualism, but a succession of haphazard, scrappy and farcical incidents, and degenerated into mere happy-go-lucky, aimless kick, rush in this exhibition.

With regard to the rule change which reduced the number of players per team from fifteen to thirteen, this was clearly a move that was designed to make the game faster and more exciting by creating more free space on the field. The ability of the Rugby League authorities to implement rapid rule changes has sometimes been seen as a major strength by their counterparts in association football, in which code, because of its international reach, it is much more difficult to enact rule changes. However, this ability is both a strength and a weakness for the sport. It is a strength because it allows the authorities to act quickly when a rule is being exploited in a manner which has a damaging effect on the game as a spectator sport. A good example of this may be taken from the 1960s when Bradford Northern, having signed Terry Price, began to use his enormous kicking power to kick the ball beyond the dead ball line without a bounce, in the knowledge that the opposing team would have to return the ball to them via a drop kick from the twenty five yard line. The Rugby League authorities acted speedily to enact the rule which penalised any attacking team which kicked the ball over the dead ball line without a bounce. The downside of this ability to change the rules quickly is that if it is done too frequently and without careful thought, it both causes confusion and leads to unintended consequences.

The latter is a charge that is frequently levelled at the rule makers of the modern game, but as may be seen from an article in the *Yorkshire Post*, 9th January, 1906, the same issue was current then: "Leigh footballers consider the Northern Union are legislating clubs out of existence with severe penalties for slight offences , and this and constant tampering with the rules are responsible for the loss of public support."

The *Yorkshire Evening Post*, 12th January 1907, in its analysis of attendances at matches, reinforced this point about a loss of public support by demonstrating that crowd numbers had fallen significantly in recent months, observing that "it shows that the public have been alienated from the game to a great extent." The balance between innovation and stability is one that is not easily achieved and it is an issue with which the modern game continues to struggle.

A Change in Fortunes: 1908-1914

Season 1907-1908 was one in which Johnny Nearey, Willie Hirst, Alfred Petty and Eddie Ward made their debuts for Batley, and was much more successful for the club than the previous campaign. Batley won nineteen of their thirty two league fixtures and lost thirteen, failing to register a score on only two occasions. By February 1908 Batley were in the top eight of the League. The *Yorkshire Evening Post*, 4th February 1908, covering the match in which Batley beat Wakefield by eighteen points to eleven, under the heading "Sensational Try by Will Davies", waxed lyrical about the performance of the Batley team, highlighting the effective teamwork of the Batley players which enabled Will Davies to score a hat trick. His final try was given particular attention: "Will Davies then scored a sensational try. Receiving the ball on his own '25', he dodged Bennett and Lynch , and easily out-distancing his pursuers, he scored." The *Hull Daily Mail*, 29th February 1908, reported that a black cat had been sent to Batley Football Club in order to bring good luck in the Northern Union cup-ties. Unfortunately, it did not have the desired effect as Batley were knocked out by Wakefield in the second round.

Batley's final match of the 1907-1908 season, against Huddersfield at Mount Pleasant, turned out to be a rum affair. As a result of players sent off or injured, Batley, who won by thirteen points to eleven, finished the game with nine men against Huddersfield's ten. The *Yorkshire Evening Post*, 13th April 1908, commented on the game as follows:

This match at Batley seems to have been a disgraceful affair. The report of the game, indeed, reminds one rather of the prize-ring than the football field. We read:-

Barker (Huddersfield) was seen indulging in foul tactics, and was sent off the field. Shortly afterwards Petty and Sykes were sent off for fighting, and Ward (Batley) received marching orders for kicking. Oakland had been injured in a rush, and when the half-time whistle blew Batley had ten men on the field and Huddersfield eleven men.

In the second half each side lost another man, Senior (Batley) having to be carried off hurt, and Brook (Huddersfield) being sent off for rough play.

Seven players made their debut for Batley during the 1908-1909 season, but of those seven only two players, Harry Thomas and Leonard Sangster, made a substantial number of appearances. However, from the outset the latter had caught the eye of the *Athletic News* which made the following observation in its edition on 31st August, 1908: "The catch of the season, however, is a sprightly young gentleman named Leonard Sangster, who hails from Huddersfield. At practice he both surprised and delighted the club managers by his all-round ability. He is only 22 years old, stands 5ft. 11in., and weighs 12 stone. His position is centre, a point which is supposed to represent Batley's weakest link."

The other good news for Batley was that Jim Gath returned to Mount Pleasant after nearly eight seasons at Hull KR. Gath, widely considered to be one of the best players of his generation, was obtained at a bargain price, a fact that was not lost on Hull KR's supporters, as the *Yorkshire Evening Post*, 5th September 1908, pointed out: "Some of the Rovers' supporters are rather indignant with the directors in allowing Gath to return to Batley for such an insignificant amount as £15. Said one ex-official the other day, "Why, he was often worth that in one match!".... The Rovers paid the Batley club £75 when Gath first came to Hull.

As promising as the recruitment of Sangster and Gath was the substantial increase in membership which took place at the beginning of the season. The addition of approximately 150 names to the subscription list constituted a record for the club. The *Batley News*, 9th October 1908, noted that forty new members had been enrolled on the previous Saturday, bringing the total to more than 850. The *Yorkshire Evening Post*, 10th October 1908, commented on the importance of this development: "A roll of between 800 and 900 members for a town of 30,000 inhabitants, so close to the headquarters of another League club as Batley is to Dewsbury, is highly satisfactory, and testifies to the hold that Rugby still retains in the Heavy Woollen district."

It seems that the threat from Association football had been repelled and the *Yorkshire Evening Post*, in the above edition, was effusive in its praise of those who had managed the financial crisis at the club: "The Batley Executive deserve well. With a debt of nearly £1,000 some three years ago, it seemed as if the club would have to go into liquidation, but by herculean efforts the liabilities have been largely reduced and if the promise of a good season is realised this winter the organisation will be once more placed on a sound footing."

1908-1909, during which Batley won all of their home games apart from one against Huddersfield which was drawn, proved to be a very successful season for the club. The icing on the cake was a victory by twelve points to five against the Australian touring team in January 1909. The surprise was that the game was only watched by 2,500 spectators, though this may have been occasioned by the conditions in which the match was played, as noted in the *Bolton Evening News*, 12th January 1909: "The weather was bitterly cold and a stiff breeze blew down the field." Those who have braved the winter conditions at Mount Pleasant will understand exactly why there was a relatively small crowd there on that day. The *Batley News*, 15th January 1909, summed up the game as follows:

The game was an interesting one to watch, being full of incident. Batley won by twelve points to five and they gained their victory by the superior tactics they adopted. The Australians are evidently a well-trained side with plenty of staying power, but of the tricks of the game they know very little. They threw the ball about enough, but the passing was flashy and rash on several occasions. The backs lack the ability of making straight dashes to the line, their main idea being to look around and make certain that there is someone to whom the ball can be passed.

The Kangaroos' attempt to win by playing an open and expansive game failed. Of course, the climatic conditions massively favoured the home side, but the importance of the victory should not be underestimated. In the early part of the following season the *Leigh Chronicle and Weekly District Advertiser*, 8th October 1909, contained an interesting snippet about Batley's winger/centre, Will Davies: "Batley are not certain whether Will T. Davies, their fast centre, who secured the sensational try against Leigh last year, will be able to play, as he was injured jumping over a player last Saturday."

Billy Batten, famous for leaping over tacklers, had made his debut for Hunslet in 1907, so it is interesting to speculate as to whether Will Davies was copying Batten or whether Batten had picked up the technique from players like Davies. By November 1909 Batley had progressed to the semi-final of the Yorkshire Cup, in which they faced Wakefield at Mount Pleasant. This game was drawn before

Batley defeated their opponents by eleven points to three in the replay. The *Yorkshire Post*, 18th November 1909 said of the replay that "Batley played the stronger and faster game", whilst the *Y.E.P.*, on the previous day, concluded its detailed report of the game with the comment that: "If Huddersfield think they have an easy thing in the final, they may, on today's Batley form find themselves mistaken."

Unfortunately, as it turned out, this prediction was wide of the mark as Batley failed to register a score in the Yorkshire Cup Final on 27th November 1909, as Huddersfield thrashed them by twenty one points to nil. Whilst Batley's presence in the final was a surprise to most followers of the game in Yorkshire, the *Hull Daily Mail*, 27th November 1909, cautioned against any attempt to write off their chances: "They are a team of veterans who have made the name of Batley feared by all opponents in cup-tie warfare. They have specialised in Cup competition football with the most satisfactory results, results which see them enter today's match with the greatest confidence."

However, a later report in the same newspaper of the actual match concluded that: "The Batley forwards were masters in the pack, but once the ball got loose Huddersfield were clearly the better side." Though it was a heavy defeat for the "Gallant Youths", they were beaten by a team that espoused a very attacking style of rugby, a team that soon became known as "the team of all talents", a team which won all four major trophies in 1915. The loss was keenly felt, but there was no shame in losing to opponents of this calibre. Batley finished the season mid-table, their away form being their Achilles heel. The difference between Batley's performances home and away during the 1909-1910 season was a subject of comment in the *Hull Daily Mail*, 1st March 1910: "It is rather singular that Batley have not won a League match away during this season. The "Gallant Youths" are holy terrors at their sloping ground at Mount Pleasant, as is evidenced by the fact that Batley have not lost a game there within the past two seasons."

The newspaper was not quite accurate in its reporting of Batley's record away from Mount Pleasant because they had, in fact, beaten Merthyr Tydfil away from home. However, it was true that Batley's last defeat at home had been in March 1908, in a cup-tie against Wakefield. At the start of the new season, 1910-1911, the *Yorkshire Post*, 28th September 1910 reported that a new insurance scheme for players had been adopted by the majority of clubs, including Batley, in the Northern Rugby League. Obviously, it was very important, as it still is today, for semi-professional players to have the security of insurance cover should they suffer an injury which prevented them from doing their day job for any length of time. The Batley Committee had sought to strengthen the team for the new season by signing Bill Anderson, a half-back, from Hull for a fee of £175. Unfortunately, Anderson did not fulfil expectations, scoring only six tries in fifty two appearances for the club, so it is perhaps no surprise that he was placed on the transfer list in October 1911. He saw out the season but he was gone by the start of the next one. As early as 26th November 1910, the *Sheffield Star*'s *Green 'Un*, not noted for its extensive coverage of rugby league, noted that "Anderson, the ex-Hull man, for whom Batley paid £175, has not done anything particularly brilliant for the 'Gallant Youths' so far." The newspaper also hints that he was carrying a leg injury, so it may be that this was the root cause of his failure to live up to his reputation as a top class half-back.

In March 1911 Batley played Salford in the quarter final of the Challenge Cup, comprehensively beating their opponents by eighteen points to three. The *Leeds Mercury*, 20th March 1911, was effusive in its praise for Batley's performance, notwithstanding its disappointment with Salford's efforts:

Playing on their own ground (Salford) it was expected that they would at least make a great fight, but as it turned out they never played like winners, and were practically routed in every position....

The Batley club has benefited from the blending of good young ones with good old ones. Youth supplies the dash and the veterans furnish the experience, – and so Batley has a team capable of rising to its greatest heights on occasions when success is of the utmost importance. There is nothing like the knock-out system for bringing out the grit that is in a man and in a team.

This blend of youth and experience included such redoubtable veterans as Wattie Davies and Jim Gath alongside younger players like Walter Drummond, Jim Lyons and James Debney. However, on this occasion Batley's renowned cup-fighting spirit was not sufficient to carry them through to the final, as they lost to Wigan by four points to two in the semi-final. During the period 1912-1915, out of one hundred and twelve fixtures Batley won fifty five, drew five and lost fifty two, failing to score on fourteen occasions, nine of which occurred during the 1914-1915 season. Amongst those who made their debuts during this period were Jack Brooksby, Ivor Bevan, 'Dowdy' Brannan, Simon Broadhead, Robert Randerson and Jack Tindall, the latter two being subsequently killed during the First World War. Once again, in January 1912, Batley played against an overseas team, beating a combined team from Australasia by thirteen points to five. The *Manchester Evening Courier*, 29th January 1912, noted that: "In the first place a large crowd, who had complained at a shilling being charged for admission rushed the gates…" In addition to provoking some fans to gain free entry, the hike in the admission charge also caused some to stay at home. In the end only 2,886 people paid for admission, a significantly smaller number than might have been expected, though an increase on the 2,500 who attended the game against Australia in January 1909. The *Reporter*, 2nd February 1912, contained a detailed report of the game, from which the following extracts have been taken:

The game was so full of exciting incidents that the spectators were kept on the jump all the time…. Batley's passing movements, generally speaking, were more frequent, better timed and considerably more useful than those on the other side, though there was not quite so much promiscuous flinging the ball about by Batley as occurred on the other side. The victors played fine, robust, exhilarating football, and were worth every point they scored, and a good many more on the day's play.

Some time ago it was pointed out by a journalistic admirer of the Australasians that the great feature of the Colonials' play was their 'finishing ten minutes'. He pointed out that there was hardly a team in the world that could stand the onslaught which the visitors were in the habit of making during the last few minutes of the game. These tactics were tried on Saturday, and certainly a less desperate team than Batley would have crumbled to pieces before the pressure which was exerted against them. But Batley stiffened their backs, and not only did they drive the enemy back after once having felt the grip of its teeth, as it were, but they carried the war into the Colonial citadel, and added to their score, a thing that is possibly unique in the Australasians' tour.

No doubt the reader will note the militaristic language used in the latter part of the second extract, a feature which is, perhaps, not too surprising given the contemporary international context of Anglo-German tension and gunboat diplomacy.

After eleven years without a trophy, Batley finally won the Yorkshire Cup in November 1912, when they met Hull in the final. The *Hull Daily Mail*, 18th November 1912, had been bullish about Hull's chances of lifting the trophy on 23rd November, whilst acknowledging that Batley's fans, many of whom had turned up to watch Hull play Dewsbury at Crown Flatt on 16th November, were supremely confident of victory. A slight whiff of schadenfreude may be detected in this newspaper's reporting of the fact that Batley would be deprived of the services of Debney and Tom Parker in the final, both having been sent off during the previous Saturday's game against Halifax. In the end their absence did not matter as Batley, in front of a crowd of 20,000 spectators, outclassed their opponents, securing a victory by seventeen points to three. The *Sheffield Star Green 'Un*, 23rd November 1912, described the way in which Hull held on until half-time but then subsequently succumbed to a speedier and stronger team. The *Reporter*, 29th November 1912, in describing the reception given to the team on its return to Batley, highlighted the fact that in recent years the fans had been starved of success, making this victory was all the sweeter:

There were scenes of the wildest excitement and enthusiasm in Batley on Saturday night, and not in recent years, at any rate, has the football fever reached such a desperate height. Though in former days bringing home the cup to Batley became almost a matter of course, the younger generation of football followers has not had an opportunity of enthusing to such an extent before, and the fact that on several occasions they have been very near a cup without actually handling it made them all the more demonstrative when on Saturday the "Gallant Youths" once more justified their title.

In the wake of Batley's triumph, the club committee announced a scheme to erect a new covered stand, as reported in the *Yorkshire Post*, 21st June 1913: "Batley Cricket and Football Club's proposed new covered stand, to accommodate 1,800 spectators, is to cost £600, of which £250 has already been raised."

The same newspaper, 29th September 1913, covered the actual opening of the new stand at the game against Huddersfield, 27th September 1913:

The Batley ground presented a gay appearance on account of the festivities associated with the opening of their new covered stand, and the "gate" was the largest that has been taken at Mount Pleasant in a League match for years, the receipts being over £240.

The covered stand erected by Batley Football Club at Mount Pleasant, at a cost of £700, towards which £400 has been raised, was opened by Mr. W. Fillan, of Huddersfield, Vice-President of the Northern Union, who was presented with a smoking-cabinet as a souvenir of the occasion.

The Mayor of Batley (Alderman S. Ward) who unfurled a new flag, given by the President of the club (Mr. Samuel Brearley) received a cigar case and holder, and Mr. Brearley was the recipient of a fountain pen.

Within a year Britain was at war with Germany, a conflict which would turn out to be a far more protracted affair than many of the participants had anticipated at the outset. The full impact of the war on Batley C.A and F.C. will be dealt with in the ensuing chapter, but the *Yorkshire Evening Post*, 7th February 1914, in its coverage of the game between Batley and Bradford Northern, under the heading "Debney Gives Magnificent Display", highlighted the performance of one of

Batley's star players who, tragically, did not make it through the war. According to the *Y.E.P*, Debney was irrepressible, running, tackling and passing in a manner which constantly put Bradford on the defensive. They had no answer to Debney's speed and energy, in the end conceding six tries whilst failing to register a single point. Britain declared war on Germany in August 1914 and at the end of the 1914-1915 season competitive games within the Northern Union were suspended, not recommencing until January 1919. Already by December 1914 Batley was beginning to feel the effects of the government's commitment to 'total war'. The *Leeds Mercury*, 21st December 1914 reported that:

If there is not a speedy and substantial improvement in the public support given to football at Mount Pleasant, the Batley club might soon find itself in an awkward financial position. Of course, a good deal of the falling off in patronage is due to the fact that many people are employed on Saturdays in the local mills, making khaki and soldiers' uniforms.

Batley C.A. and F.C. may have been damaged by the war, in a number of ways, but some mill owners were able to make a tidy profit.

Controversy and Unwelcome Publicity

Whilst there were peaks and troughs in the team's performances 1900-1915, Batley C.A. and F.C., like many other clubs, had to deal with controversial issues and handle unwelcome publicity during this period. In March 1900 Batley was fined £25 by the Yorkshire Senior Competition Committee as a result of an attack on the referee following a game against Halifax on the 24th February. Mr. Marshall, the match referee, sent a letter to the Secretary of the Yorkshire

Senior Competition, from which the following extract has been taken:

Immediately on leaving the field, I was struck in the face with a hard piece of earth, and on approaching the Batley dressing-room I was struck several times with stones on the back of my head and body; also some of the officials who were trying to protect me were struck, one having his lip cut open by a stone.

The *Reporter,* 9th March 1900, thought that the fine was excessive, in the light of the fact that Castleford had been fined a similar amount for a second offence of this nature, whereas this was Batley's first appearance in front of the committee for what the newspaper described as "referee baiting". Whether this term was the one used by the committee or whether it was the newspaper's own is not clear, but either way it does appear to be a euphemism for what was a straightforward assault on the referee. As was recorded in the previous chapter, it was not unknown for individual members of the Batley team to fall foul of the law. The *Yorkshire Evening Post,* 7th March 1902, noted that Charlie Stubley, Batley's well known and very well regarded forward, was fined ten shillings plus costs for allowing a lottery to take place on his licensed premises, the Clarence Inn, Commercial Street, Batley. Charlie Stubley denied the charge, but it seems that an undercover police officer provided eye witness testimony which convinced the magistrates that the defendant was guilty.

The following year, as reported in both the *Batley News,* 20th March 1903, and the *Yorkshire Post,* 21st March 1903, the club was mired in controversy as accusations were made that the recent matches against Barrow and Halifax had been "sold" i.e. deliberately lost as a consequence of bribery. The rugby correspondent in the *Batley News* considered the claims of bribery to be little more than malicious gossip, though he acknowledged that there were divisions within the team, divisions which had led to open quarrelling on the field and blows being struck in the dressing-room. In the end, following what the *Batley News* described as a" thorough investigation", the club committee concluded that no corruption or bribery had taken place.

Once again, in September 1904, a match referee was assaulted at the end of a game at Mount Pleasant. Following a closely fought game against Wigan on 24th September 1904, during which two Batley tries were disallowed, the referee was struck on the head by a missile as he made his way back to the dressing-rooms. On this occasion, The Yorkshire Senior Competition Committee, having received a full report of the incident, decided to suspend Batley's ground from competition for a month. The consequence was that Batley had to play two of their home games on neutral grounds, Bradford Park Avenue and Belle Vue, Wakefield respectively.

Somewhat more seriously, an incident which occurred at the end of Batley's match against Leeds at Mount Pleasant, 31st December 1904, led to a court case. The *Yorkshire Evening Post*, 13th January 1905, reported that:

Leeds forward Elijah Watts was charged with assault at Batley Police Court. Watts was summoned for assaulting Wharton Peers Davies, the well-known Batley threequarter. The allegation was that as the players were leaving the field Watts dealt Davies a violent blow in the face.

Prosecutor Pearson said because of the rough play the spectators got very angry. The crowd was so angry with Watts that he needed police protection on the way to the dressing room. However, he broke away from the Police Inspector and struck Davies from behind. The assault may have led to a serious riot. Watts was pulled off Davies and taken away by Detective Higgins and the Inspector. The present summons was issued at the request of the Police and the Batley Football Club.

According to the *Batley News*, 13th January 1905, Watts, when cross examined, denied that he had either committed acts of violence during the game or struck Davies en route to the dressing-room, claiming that he had been the victim of an assault by one of the Batley players during the game. Unsurprisingly, the Court chose to believe the evidence of the police officers who said that they had witnessed the assault and Watts was fined twenty shillings plus costs. One of the most noticeable features of the sport during this period is the violent nature of the games. It is almost as though each team's approach to a match was predicated on the assumption that at least one of their players would be sent off for violent conduct. In James Sharpe's marvellous book about the history of violence in England, *A Fiery and Furious People* (Random House, 2016), the author notes that "In the years immediately before the First World War at least one insurance company is known to have refused to insure players in the recently formed Rugby League."

The *Yorkshire Evening Post*, 16th February 1910 and *Batley News* 18th February 1910, both contained reports of what appears to have been an extremely violent game between Batley and Hull KR, in which no fewer than four players were sent off, three from Hull KR and one from Batley. The former newspaper observed that: "Hull KR reported the referee for incompetence, and both they and Batley sent deputations to support their players who had been reported for roughness."

All this was to no avail, because the Northern Rugby

League committee, having refused to take testimony from the deputations, imposed suspensions on those four players who had been dismissed. When Batley played Keighley on 15th February 1913, following an altercation between James Debney (Batley) and Buckley (Keighley) which had occurred during the match, the latter entered the Batley dressing-room and struck the former from behind, knocking him out, whilst he was in the bath. Though this was undoubtedly a prima facie case of assault, it seems that neither the club nor Debney pursued the matter!

Some events which generated unwelcome publicity for Batley C.A. and F.C. were beyond the club's immediate control. The *Yorkshire Post*, 16th April 1912, contained the following story under the heading "Football Fixtures and False Pretences":

Edwin Ward, baker, pleaded guilty to obtaining six shillings by false pretences, the money of L. Wood at Dewsbury, on February 20th, and obtaining eight shillings from Mr. E. Wood, at Dewsbury on February 22nd. Mr. Beverley, prosecuting, said that the prisoner had presented himself a representative of the Batley Football Club – and was letting spaces in fixture cards – taking money for the purpose of inserting advertisements in the cards.

The perpetrator, who had already been convicted and imprisoned for a similar offence in Bradford, was sentenced to eighteen months in prison to run concurrently with the previous sentence. The same newspaper, 28th December 1912, contained an article about a more tragic incident which had occurred during Batley's Boxing Day fixture against Dewsbury at Crown Flatt. Unfortunately, Herbert Foster Marriot, a young Dewsbury fan who suffered from Bright's disease (a kidney complaint), having become excited after

Dewsbury had kicked a penalty, collapsed and died. The *Yorkshire Post* reported that the surgeon who had carried out the post-mortem on the deceased "was of the opinion that Marriot had died from a rupture(due to excitement) of a diseased blood vessel in the brain and Bright's disease, from which he was suffering."

In the modern era we are used to details of the private lives of sporting personalities being splashed across the newspapers, but this phenomenon was more unusual in the early part of the twentieth century. However, the *Yorkshire Evening Post*, 18th July 1913, under the headline "Home Life of a Batley Footballer", reported that Batley's full back, James Lyons, had been in court because his wife was seeking a separation order on the grounds of desertion. She claimed that when she left her in-law's house, where she, James Lyons and her children had lived, because they drank, James had promised to join her, but had failed to do so. James, having told the court that he was completely teetotal and that he had always handed over all of his wages to his wife, explained why he had not joined his wife. The newspaper, perhaps for reasons of propriety, declined to specify what James Lyons had said, but noted that the magistrates "made a maintenance order for ten shillings a week, and the wife to be given custody of the children."

Rugby Union in Batley

By 1914 Rugby League, notwithstanding some hiccups along the way, was firmly established as the premier sport in Batley. However, Rugby Union continued to be played in the town and the *Yorkshire Evening Post*, 1st July 1902 reported that the Batley Rugby Union Club had, the previous evening, been formally admitted to membership of the Yorkshire Rugby Union. Somewhat surprisingly, given the generally acrimonious relations between the Rugby Union and those clubs which had seceded in 1895, Batley Rugby Union team was given permission by the Rugby Union committee, as reported in the *Yorkshire Post*, 17th March 1903, to replay a cup-tie against Kirkstall Congregational at the "Batley Northern Union" ground. Perhaps at a local level there had been a thaw in the normally frosty relations between the codes, possibly as a result of personal connections between the two clubs.

In 1907, it has already been noted, there was a mini-crisis within the Northern Union, precipitated by disquiet caused by rule changes, and there was even talk of the possibility of reunion with the Rugby Union. This did not, of course occur, and it is certain, as indicated by the Rugby Union's investigation into "veiled professionalism", reported in the *Sheffield Daily Telegraph*, 14th January 1907, that in any discussions about reunification between the Rugby Union and the Northern Union the former would have wanted to call the shots. In 1912, according to the Yorkshire Post, Batley Rugby Union Club was playing matches at Carlton Grange, Batley, but the *Yorkshire Evening Post*, 7th March 1914, noted that Batley Rugby Union Club had been disbanded, allowing Otley a walk-over in the first round of the Yorkshire Cup Competition. The club did subsequently re-form, but never challenged the supremacy of Batley C. A. and F. C.

Cricket at Mount Pleasant

Lest it be forgotten that Batley Rugby Football Club was founded as an adjunct to the cricket club, it is important to note that the latter was still flourishing in the early part of the twentieth century. In fact the successes of the cricket team acted as a useful counterbalance when the rugby team was in the doldrums in the early 1900s. The *Leeds Mercury*, 10th January 1906, reported that:

At the annual social of the Batley C. A. and F. Club last night in the Town Hall, the Mayor of Batley (Alderman George Hirst) presented medals to the members of the Cricket Team which in the season 1905 won the Heavy Woollen Challenge Cup. Mr. Hirst also presented a marble timepiece and barometer to Mr. Herbert Robinson, a member of the first eleven, whose abilities as a batsman contributed largely to its success....

The *Yorkshire Evening Post*, 9th September 1911, included an article, replete with statistics, about Batley Cricket Club's victory against Hopton Mills in the Heavy Woollen Cup Final. Apparently, this had been a record breaking match with an aggregate of 728 runs scored on the day, 445 of which had been scored by Batley. The team captain, Arthur Crowther, whose batting average for the season was 78.5, had scored 231 not out, the highest score ever made in a final up to that date. The *Yorkshire Post*, 20th July 1914, recorded how rugby football and cricket came together at Mount Pleasant in its report of a "benefit" cricket match arranged for Wattie Davies:

The interesting local match between Batley and Birstall was set apart for "Wattie" Davies, the Welshman, who, as footballer and cricketer has served the Batley club right worthily for eighteen years. In a dramatic and most exciting finish the Mount Pleasant team won by one wicket, and it was the excitement towards the finish that the beneficiary ran himself out after scoring seven.

This account, of course, highlights the fact that during this period many rugby players played cricket in the off-season, some of them at a very high level.

Community Activities at Mount Pleasant

Throughout the early 1900s Mount Pleasant continued to be used for a variety of activities other than official rugby and cricket matches. The *Leeds Mercury*, 27th January 1902, noted that Walter Runciman, the Liberal candidate in the local parliamentary by-election "addressed three splendid meetings in Batley on Saturday afternoon and evening. At the close of the football match at Mount Pleasant, a large crowd assembled to hear Mr. Runciman near the football field." In the same year, the Lancashire Military Tournament, involving a display of strength and skill, was also held at Mount Pleasant, footage of which is held in the B.F.I. archive. Similarly, a schools pageant was held at the ground in 1907, whilst in the *Reporter*'s discussions about the possibility of an Association football team being established in Batley, 22nd February 1907, the newspaper makes reference to the fact that a hockey club was playing matches at Mount Pleasant.

Charity activities, it seems, were not infrequent events at Batley's ground and the *Yorkshire Evening Post*, 24th November 1908, recorded one such event:

A Charity Football match between teams got together by "Wattie" Davies and Mr. R. N. Wheatley of Mirfield, attracted a good crowd to Mount Pleasant, Batley, this afternoon. "Wattie" Davies played on the wing and included in his side were Will Davies and Jack Rodgers (the old Batley forward) .... Jack Rodgers, whose weight is eighteen stones, was at half-back. There were many amusing incidents in the match.

As indicated in the previous chapter, the Batley Show became an annual fixture for many years at Mount Pleasant, and the *Leeds Mercury*, 24th May 1909, included a lengthy article about that year's event:

The Australian cricket team which played against a Batley and District X1 in 1878

An advertisement for a Batley away game against Llanelli in 1885

Richard Webster (aka 'London Dick'), the trainer of Batley's team which won the Yorkshire Challenge Cup in 1885

Leaflet from The Rugby League Museum Society of New Zealand – photo of the teams before the 1897 Cup Final

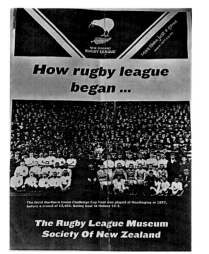

George Main in 1938 with his former teammates from the 1897-1901 era (*courtesy of Batley News and Reporter*). Back row (*left to right*): R. Roberts (*Batley News*), A. Garner, J. Brearley, J. Sheard (*Reporter*). Middle row (left to right): J. Littlewood, D Fitzgerald, J. Oakland, J. B. Goodall, W. P. Davies, E. Kirk. Front row (*left to right*): R. Barraclough, J. H. Phillips, J. Gath, G. Main, F. W. H. Auty, R. Spurr, J. F. Whitaker

Three elderly 'Gallant Youths': Wattie Davies, Jim Gath and George Main in 1957 (courtesy of *The Batley News*)

Wattie Davies tees up a kick in the 1901 Cup Final

Batley Schools' Pageant at Mount Pleasant 1907

Frank Gallagher, *above*

Wattie Davies in uniform
during World War One

Batley team 1924 – winners of two trophies (courtesy of *A 'Ton' Full of Memories*,
Brian Cartwright 1986). Back row (*left to right*): A. Armitage (trainer), A. Brooke,
J. Gledhill, F. Carter, S. Smith, G. Armitage, G. Douglas, G. Ramsbottom.
Middle row (*left to right*): W. Rees, G. Davidge, W. Scott, I. J. Fowler (Cpt.),
J. Robinson, H. R. Rees, H. Murray, G. Thwaites (trainer)
Front row (*left to right*): B. Williams, A. Carter

The Batley veterans team that played a police team in a 1926 charity match.
Can you spot Jim Gath, Jack Goodall and Wattie Davies?

Invite to Official
Dinner after game
at Mount Pleasant
between Australian
Air Force XV and a
French Air Force
XV, February 1945
Right: Bill Riches

A Supporters' Club dance in 1938 (*courtesy of Batley Reporter*)

George Palmer in action and at a reunion, *below right*, with, Bill Riches, seated left. Standing (*left to right*): Jack Perry, Jeff Stevenson, John Etty. *Inset*: Norman Field

Ticket for a Supporters' Club dinner and social 1954 (*courtesy of Bill Winner*)

Batley team February 1964 (*courtesy of Yorkshire Sports and Football Argus*) Back row (*left to right*): Bateson, Fryer, Dick, Sharp, Kennedy, Noble Front row (*left to right*): Hammond, Shuttleworth, Geldard, Smith, Ward, Foster, Oliver. Mascot: Billy Settle

Supporter's Club committee mid-1970s (*courtesy of Bill Winner*).
Back row (*left to right*): Barry Lee, Trevor Heylings, Bill Winner, Stephen Boden.
Middle row: (*left to right*) Michael ?, Norman Coop, Jack Walker, Laurie Gott,
Harry Myers. Front row (*left to right*): Elaine ?, John Winner, Ruth Hinchcliffe.

Ruth Hinchcliffe subsequently became Ruth Boden, but was still known as
Ruth Hinchcliffe when the photograph was taken. The surname of Michael and
Elaine (husband and wife) remain unknown.

A page from the
Supporters' Club
Minute Book
1974 (*courtesy of
Bill Winner*)

Pictured right:
Tommy Martyn

Programme
for Batley v
Fulham
Centenary
match, 1981

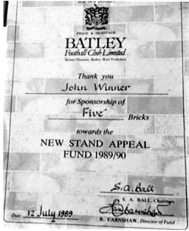

New Stand Appeal Fund Certificate 1989-1990 (*courtesy of Bill Winner*)

Official Programme, Northern Rail Cup Final 2010, *right*

Karl Harrison: coach of Batley's Northern Rail Cup Final team, *left*

Simon Wilson in action, *right*, and signing for Batley, *below* (*both images courtesy of Batley News*)

First Inductees to the Hall of Fame, November 2019: (*left to right*) Simon Wilson,
John Etty, Carl Gibson, Alan Almond (on behalf of Ike Fowler)

Ike Fowler, *above*, Carl Gibson,
below, and John Etty, *right*

The enclosure at Mount Pleasant presented an animated sight with about ten thousand spectators watching the judging....

The bulldogs were a strong section, and included some really classical dogs. Mr. J. B. Whiteley of Bradford, secured two firsts with his Bill Sikes, a young dog who has not been shown much, but which is almost a perfect type, and more to be heard of in future....

The gate receipts for the day amounted to £150, which was almost £20 less than last year, but the subscriptions were considerably increased, and this accounted for the decrease in the admission receipts, the total being in advance of last year.

In fact, the local Agricultural Society, which organised Batley Show, contributed £100 towards the construction of the new covered stand in 1913 on condition that the Society had free use of the ground for the next eight years, and for £10 per year afterwards. In summer 1912 the Annual Hospital Sports event, promoted by the Batley and District Amateur Athletic Association, was held at Mount Pleasant in front of approximately seven thousand spectators. The *Yorkshire Evening Post*, 17th June 1912, covered the occasion:

Brilliant weather prevailed, and the grass course, about a quarter of a mile in circumference, was in splendid condition...

The leading features were the half-mile cycle scratch race for the Talbot Memorial Trophy; 600 yards workmens' relay race for the Jessop Challenge Bowl; the mile cycle Championship of the West Riding and a short-limit 100 yards handicap.

The money raised was for the benefit of Batley Hospital, a good illustration of the way in which Batley C. A. and F. C. was both willing and able to accommodate events which were of benefit to the local community.

From Triumph to Trauma

TIMELINE: 1915–1930
UK and World Events

1915 –   German Zeppelins bomb towns in East Anglia
         The Lusitania is sunk by a German torpedo
1916 –   Rasputin is murdered by Russian noblemen
         The Battle of the Somme
1917 –   The Russian Revolution
         The Battle of Passchendaele
1918 –   The Representation of the People Act is passed
         The First World War ends
1919 –   Prohibition commences in the USA
         The Amritsar Massacre
1920 –   The League of Nations is founded
         Metropolitan Police Flying Squad established
1921 –   Car tax discs are introduced in the UK
         Chanel No. 5 perfume is created by Coco Chanel
1922 –   Mussolini seizes power in Italy
         The Irish Free State comes into existence
1923 –   Wembley Stadium is opened to the public
         Hitler's Beer Hall Putsch fails
1924 –   The first Labour Government is elected in the UK
         First Winter Olympics held in Chamonix, France
1925 –   John Logie Baird transmits first television pictures
         The Great Gatsby by F. Scott Fitzgerald is published
1926 –   The General Strike takes place in Britain
         The chemical company ICI is created
1927 –   The BBC is granted a Royal Charter
         Lindbergh completes first solo transatlantic flight
1928 –   Alexander Fleming discovers Penicillin
         The first Harry Ramsden's fish and chip shop opens
1929 –   The first Tesco opens, in Middlesex
         The Wall Street Crash occurs

5

WORLD WAR ONE AND ITS AFTERMATH – PEAKS AND TROUGHS: 1915-1930

The Immediate Impact of WW 1

The written word can scarcely do justice to the suffering, physical, emotional and psychological, experienced by the British nation both during and in the aftermath of the First World War. The impact of this devastating conflict affected all areas of social life, rugby league being no exception. Chris and Jane Roberts, in their wonderful book, *The Greatest Sacrifice* (Scratching Shed, Sept. 2018), have charted in detail the individual stories of all the first team professional rugby league players who lost their lives in the Great War, but a brief reflection on the five Batley players amongst that number is necessary here. Batley lost five of its players as a result of the war: Joseph Child; James Debney; Walter Johnson; Robert Randerson and Jack Tindall. The first two named had made their debut in 1909, Tindall in 1912, whilst Johnson and Randerson had only just made their first team appearances in 1914. The *Leeds Mercury*, 15th May 1915, reported Jack Tindall's death in a brief, but poignant, article:

Jack Tindall, the well-known Batley three-quarter has been killed in action. He was one of a party who volunteered to take rations to some of the R.F.A., and were unable to return to their company. They took shelter in a trench, but a shell struck the trench and Tindall was killed. He was buried near the spot by his comrades, and a little wooden cross was placed over his grave. He was in the Leeds Rifles, 8th Battallion.

Though the official competition was suspended at the end of the 1914-1915 season and did not recommence until January 1919, unofficial matches were played during the interim period, with many teams making use of 'guest' players. As we shall see, this was in contrast to arrangements during World War 2 when the official competition continued, in spite of the very widespread use of 'guest' players by most teams, none more so than Batley. The wartime league 1915-1918 was called 'The War Emergency League', but as noted by the *Yorkshire Post*, 14th February 1916, it had no official recognition as a Championship. Nonetheless, these unofficial matches were taken seriously, as the *Leeds Mercury*, 4th October 1915, recorded in its report of the derby game at Crown Flatt on the 2nd October:

On paper, Dewsbury had much the stronger side, reinforced as they were by the pick of the Wakefield team, but Batley put up a surprisingly good fight, and Dewsbury had not the runaway victory which many had expected.

The game was closely and keenly contested, and once or twice the players introduced a little unnecessary vigour, but, on the whole it was in an admirable spirit.

The *Hull Daily Mail*, 12th November 1915, in its preview of the following day's match between Hull and Batley at the Boulevard, in addition to making specific reference to one of the Hull forwards, Hammill, appearing for Batley, the newspaper noted the impact that the war had already had on the team as a result of the loss of Tindall and Randerson. Interestingly, Batley are referred to as the "Green and Whites", as opposed to the more familiar cerise and fawn with which the "Gallant Youths" were normally associated. Whether this was a change strip or a wartime contingency is not clear. Although all matches were unofficial during this period, the committees of the Northern Union were still active, making what some, considering the circumstances, may have considered to be rather pedantic rulings. The *Yorkshire Evening Post*, 20th January 1916, noted that the sub-committee of the Yorkshire Northern Union had fined Batley 18 shillings, on the basis of one shilling per minute, for a late start in their home game against Bramley on 18th December 1915. Clearly, the Northern Union was keen to ensure that its authority was not flouted during this period of unofficial competition.

The ersatz nature of Northern Union teams 1915–1918, one of the main reasons why the matches were unofficial, is revealed in the *Leeds Mercury*, 15th January 1917 and 2nd April of the same year. The former, in its report of Batley's home match against York, noted that: "York had only about half a team when they arrived at the ground, and it was only with the assistance of four Batley players:- Tom Parker; Travis; Ramsden and France – that they were able to field a full side. On the other hand, Batley were well represented, the team including Pte. Harry Hodgson , who was home on leave from the Front."

Whilst the latter newspaper, in relation to Batley's game against Bradford Northern on 31st March, reported that: "As a matter of fact, Bradford arrived with four players short, and only by borrowing a full-back, a centre and two forwards they fielded a full side."

World War One and its Aftermath

An official competition could not take place in circumstances in which teams had to lend some of their own players to their opponents in order for the matches to go ahead. Unsurprisingly, given that the First World War resulted in the full mobilisation of British society in support of the war effort, attendances and gate revenues declined during this period. The *Leeds Mercury*, 24th January 1916 and 2nd April 1917, made specific reference to a relatively small crowd at Mount Pleasant, the former estimating the number at approximately 1500. The same newspaper, 16th May 1917, included a report of the annual meeting of Batley C.A. and F.C. which stated that:

At the annual meeting of the Batley Cricket, Athletic and Football Club, last night, the president, Mr. Sam Brearley, the chairman, the Secretary, Mr. W. K. Newsome, reported a large decrease in membership and said that unless members and the public were prepared to show a more generous and loyal interest in the club, the committee were apprehensive for the future.

When many of Batley's fans were working in local textile mills producing cloth from which military uniforms were made, work which did not cease on Saturdays during the war, it was inevitable that attendances at home games would suffer. Whilst rugby matches were doubtless a welcome distraction from the horrors that were being reported from the Western Front, sport was not necessarily at the forefront of the fans' minds, most especially as casualties began to mount.

The loss of five players, though Child was no longer a regular first team member, was a major blow for the club and one from which it would take some time for it to recover. Nonetheless, the Batley Committee, with an eye to the future, continued to recruit new players during the war, as the *Yorkshire Evening Post*, 12th February 1916, noted:

Instead of rooting out old players from their retirement and permitting them to expose the physical deficiencies of crabbed age, the Batley officials have, very wisely, looked around for younger talent which may develop in War time and reach maturity when normal conditions return to an afflicted world. They have been successful in getting together a promising side, and in their two young half backs, Waterworth and Robinson, they have a pair who, with reasonable luck, are likely to be very useful to the club in the future .... the Batley management can be congratulated upon having discovered good talent and provided ample opportunities for its development.

Both the *Hull Daily Mail*, 7th February 1916 and *Yorkshire Post*, 14th February 1916, reinforced the view that in recruiting Robinson and Waterworth the Batley Committee had made a very astute move, highlighting the fact that this pair were taller and stronger than the average half-back in the Northern Union competition and thus had the potential to be Batley's best half-back pairing since the glory days of the 1890s and early 1900s. However, though both players turned out for Batley before January 1919, neither was able to make a registered debut until the Northern Union competition officially recommenced. With regard to Waterworth, once the Armistice had been signed in November 1918, there was a desire to return to normal competition as soon as possible. The *People*, 8th December 1918, observed that Batley was one of several clubs who were chomping at the bit.

World War One and its Aftermath

Rebuilding: 1919-20

The process of rebuilding the team in the wake of World War 1, a process which had begun during the course of the war, continued in its immediate aftermath. Jack Etty, Ike Fowler, Tom Harkness, George Ramsbottom, Tom Wynard and Bryn Williams all made their debuts in 1919 or 1920. The first named was the father of future Batley players John and Jim Etty, whilst Fowler, Ramsbottom and Williams became star players in their own right, between them clocking up more than 700 appearances and 600 points for the club. Fowler and Williams had been recruited from Welsh rugby union, the former having played for his country against the New Zealand All Blacks, and a player who, along with the peerless Jonty Parkin, was considered to be one of the best half-backs of his era.

The *Hull Daily Mail*, 6th February 1919, remarked on the youthful appearance of the Batley team and mused as to what specific ingredients of the town enabled it to produce so many talented forwards at so early an age. At the same time, no doubt on behalf of Batley fans, the newspaper lamented the departure to Crown Flatt of Paddy Judge, the Batley forward, who had been expected to captain the team when the official competition had recommenced in January. The *Leeds Mercury*, 23rd April 1919, described the previous day's match between Batley and Hunslet, which Batley won by eighteen points to fifteen, as a free scoring affair in which Jack Etty, playing in a clever and astute fashion, scored two tries. Of course, Jack's son, John, subsequently cemented his own reputation as one of the club's true legends, scoring more than ninety tries in almost 350 appearances for the first team. Jack was related to the 19th century English painter, William Etty, famous for his depiction of nudes, though John's artistry was of a different kind altogether.

The *Leeds Mercury*, 16th August 1919, heralded the arrival at Mount Pleasant of Isaac John Fowler, noting, presciently as it turned out, that "Fowler is probably the most important capture the Batley club has made in recent years." As one, soon to be famous, recruit arrived at The Mount, so another equally famous name departed this life. The *Yorkshire Evening Post*, 12th September 1919, recorded the death, aged sixty eight, of the very first captain of Batley Football Club, Jacob Parker, who had led the team to victory in The Yorkshire Challenge Cup Final, April 1885. The newspaper noted that: "Jake Parker, as he was familiarly known, was one of those players who helped to build the fine reputation possessed by the Batley team in its early days. He was a sturdy forward, full of dash and go, and was popular for his clean methods of play. Occasionally he played in the three quarter line."

The same newspaper, the following day, noting that Jacob Parker had also been a member of Batley Town Council, briefly reported details of his funeral: "The coffin was borne to the grave by five old footballers of the famous team which won the Cup:- Abraham Scholes, Fred Bennett, James Storer, Herbert Simms and Tom Nicholson."

It was not long before Ike Fowler began to make his mark in the sport, as the *Hull Daily Mail*, 24th October 1919, in its preview of Hull's game against Batley, observed: "Batley have also unearthed a treasure in the Welsh International half, Fowler, and it will be a right royal battle between him and the new star half, Caswell. The Welsh scrum half has improved with every match with Batley, and against Bradford last week, at Birch Lane, Fowler carried the Mount Pleasant team into the second round of the Yorkshire Cup by a brilliant scoring effort."

The newspaper, in predicting a Hull victory, drew

attention to the massive disparity, in Hull's favour, between the points scored and conceded by both teams in League games since the beginning of the season. In the event, Batley won the match by nine points to five. Batley may have had a jittery start to the 1919-20 season, but by November 1919 there was evidence that the rebuilding process was beginning to bear fruit when Batley reached the semi-final of the Yorkshire Cup, in which they lost to Leeds by sixteen points to five. Nonetheless, Batley did not disgrace themselves and, according to the *Yorkshire Post*, 17th November 1919, tested the opposition in an exciting match:

The Yorkshire Cup semi-final between Leeds and Batley produced a surprisingly fine match considering the conditions. There had been a heavy fall of snow in the early morning .... there was a "gate" of about 13,000 spectators, who enjoyed a match of thrilling incidents....

Play was at a fast pace from the start, and Batley attacked more due to their superior scrimmaging....

A ding-dong struggle followed. Batley's strong forward play made severe demands upon the Leeds defence.

In the end, it seems that the superior speed and agility of the Leeds backs was the decisive factor. Nonetheless, the rebuilding process continued apace and in January 1920, metaphorically at least, Batley signed two for the Price of one, in so far as the club signed William Price, a full-back from Pontypool, and David Price, a centre from Llanelli. The *Yorkshire Evening Post*, 24th January 1920, observed that the former, having played in war-time international rugby union matches for Wales, would almost certainly have won a full Welsh cap had he not switched codes. In the event, Bill Price made more than eighty appearances for Batley, but Dai Price only played in eight first team games before moving to Leigh. The *Hull Daily Mail*, 26th February 1920, in its preview of Batley's upcoming visit to the Boulevard, provided a very detailed analysis of the strengths and weaknesses of the newly reconstructed Batley team, drawing particular attention to the team's new style of play:

For quite a long period, the name of "Batley" was synonymous with a type of football which, though wonderfully successful, was not a spectacular feature....

Now of late, and especially during the present season, Batley, too, have come into line with those exponents of the free-handling game, and here comes the surprise, although the traditional cup-fighters have not won such match and cup successes under their new style, they have won what is more to them – public support.

This observation was, to some extent, a back-handed compliment, but the newspaper continued to wax lyrical about Batley's all-round strength in depth, noting that the transfer of Cresswell and Newsome to Hull was a clear sign that the team had sufficient cover for its regular pack, an indication of which was that a player of Simon Broadhead's ability could not secure a regular first team spot. Once again this newspaper singled out Ike Fowler for particular praise, arguing that he was the pivot around whom Batley's style of play had been transformed, a signing that was as good as any Northern Union team had made in recent years. Given the quality of the team that was being built at Batley, it is therefore no surprise that some of the players were either considered or selected for representative honours. The *Leeds Mercury*, 27th February 1920, noted that both Ike Fowler and Fred Carter had been selected to play in the upcoming trial match for the tour of Australasia, and the same newspaper,

World War One and its Aftermath

22nd October 1920, highlighted the "sterling" performance of Tom Harkness in his appearance for Yorkshire in the county match against Lancashire the previous day. The Batley committee's efforts to put together a team that would be able to compete with the best in the League did not go unnoticed, as is indicated by the following comment made in the *Yorkshire Post*, 30th October 1920, in its preview of Batley's cup-tie against Hunslet: "The Batley team, in the construction of which expense has not been spared...." Though the "Gallant Youths" lost that particular game by ten points to nine, the club's ambition was clear; it was sharply focused on the acquisition of some silverware.

Scaling new Heights 1920-25

During the period 1920-1923 a range of high quality players made their debut appearances for the first team, amongst them were: Harry Rees; Hugh Murray; Evan Rees; Willie Scott; Norman Gardiner; George Douglas; George Kilbey; William Brennan; Alonza Brook; Frank Gallagher; Albert Carter and George Davidge. Between them, the last named along with Harry Rees, Willie Scott and George Kilbey clocked up more than seven hundred appearances for Batley. Hugh Murray, a speedy South African winger, scored thirty seven tries across seventy appearances. Willie Scott, described in the *Jedburgh Gazette*, 29th July 1921, as "Jed-Forest's skilful and valued half-back", was signed from that Scottish Rugby Union Club. The prize capture in 1922, from Dewsbury, of Frank Gallagher, was recorded in the *Hull Daily Mail*, 20th October 1922, which made special reference to both the fee paid and the player's stature within the game:

The Batley Football Club, on Thursday night, signed on Frank Gallagher, the famous international forward. It is understood that

Gallagher has been transferred from Dewsbury at the exceptionally high transfer fee, for a forward, of £600. Gallagher, who is considered to be the finest loose forward in the Union, will play for Batley against Oldham on Saturday.

Gallagher's performances for Batley were inspirational and a mark of his stature within the sport may be determined from the report in the *Leeds Mercury*, 27th August 1923, in its coverage of Batley's game against Keighley, that Gallagher was dismissed for the first time in his career. Given the violent nature of the game during this period, it is quite remarkable that Gallagher had been able to maintain a clean disciplinary record up to this point. It is a clear indication of his professional self-discipline.

Instant success is very hard to come by, so the process of reconstruction was gradual as the new recruits had to gel and evolve a style of play which suited their talents. Moreover, even at this juncture, the club needed to negotiate terms with its players in order to retain their services, most especially those key players who were likely to be in demand elsewhere. The *Hull Daily Mail*, 7th September 1923, reported that Bryn Williams, Harry Rees and the formidable Fred Carter (recruited from Leeds in 1920) had all held out until the previous week in order to secure improved terms. Obviously, nowadays there is much more flux with regard to the movement of players, with the involvement of agents even below the level of Super League, but maintaining a cohesive squad of players was a delicate task as early as the 1920s.

Batley's progress was gradual. The team won or drew eighteen of the thirty four league and cup fixtures 1920-1921, twenty six of forty three 1921-1922 and twenty one of forty two 1922-1923, but within those statistics there were some sterling performances and an appearance, albeit unsuccessful, in the Yorkshire Cup Final in December 1922. One of the features of the team during this period, though this had also been true during the heydays of the 1890s, was the flexibility of the players. The *Leeds Mercury*, 10th January 1921, in its coverage of Batley's game against Halifax on the 8th January, included the following:

A couple of minutes from the close, however, Fred Carter, the ex-Leeds forward, who was playing on the right wing, created memorable scenes of enthusiasm amongst Batley's supporters by scoring a sensational try. Carter received the ball from Rees, just inside the Halifax half, and after evading one or two opponents, he kicked over the head of Garforth, and then won a thrilling race for the touch down.

Similarly, the same newspaper, 5th March 1923, in its report on Batley's defeat of St Helens Recreation, recorded that Frank Gallagher had played at stand-off and Ike Fowler at full-back. That Batley was putting together a potentially formidable team is not in doubt, a fact that is attested to by the presence in the Welsh team that played England on 19th January 1921 of the Batley players Bryn Williams and Fred Willis. The latter had made his debut in February 1920, but unfortunately moved on after a couple of seasons at the club. Batley's strength in depth was reinforced at this time by the club's 'A' team, which the *Todmorden Advertiser*, 17th November 1922, detailed in its coverage of a friendly fixture between the 'A' team and Calder Valley. Mackereth, McAvoy, Preston and Lee, all of whom are mentioned in the report, also made appearances for the first team. The importance of a reserve team should not be underestimated, but unfortunately this is a luxury that the club can no longer afford. A clear sign of the revival of Batley's fortunes came with the stunning victory against Leeds in the semi-final of the Yorkshire Cup in November 1922. Leeds, the cup holders were the clear favourites, but Batley beat them at Headingley by twenty eight points to nil, scoring six tries in the process. The *Athletic News*, 20th November 1922, was nigh on ecstatic in its praise of Batley under the heading "Batley's Brilliance":

....*the Cup-holders were thoroughly routed, and I doubt if anyone of the 25,000 spectators, who contributed £1,528, would question the result and in any degree attempt to minimise the worth of Batley's dazzling victory.*

So determined were Fowler and his comrades in attack, and so easily were the spasmodic invasions of Leeds into their half repulsed, that the result of the game never appeared in doubt after the first ten minutes....

When once the Batley backs and forwards obtained the measure of their opponents, they played sound and attractive football, and beat Leeds by movements and combination in which they are supposed to excel.

The *Leeds Mercury*, on the same date, reinforced the sentiments expressed above: "It was amazing, this wonderful inspired form of Batley's; this complete subjection of Leeds. One bears mark to the triumph; but in reality it was a tragedy to see a team of such standing not merely beaten, but slaughtered. It was the old Batley Cup-fighting policy under a new mantle, modernised; that worrying, searching, hammering, destructive force polished by a science and artistry which raised the side to the point of greatness."

Allowing for the hyperbole and excessively flowery language which tends to characterise the match reports of this era, Batley's performance in this match was clearly exceptional. It appears that it was one of those games when all the positive elements of the team fused together to produce a display of outstanding quality. Needless to say, as a consequence of this performance, The Yorkshire Cup Final in which Batley were to face York, was eagerly awaited by the press. The *Leeds Mercury*, 2nd December 1922, in its preview of the match, failed to do justice to Batley's rich history as cup fighting titans when it claimed that neither club contesting the Final had much experience of Cup warfare before. What was true is that Batley had little recent experience of contesting cup finals. Nonetheless, this newspapers's assessment was that should York score first, Batley would find it extremely difficult to break down their opponent's formidable defence. The *Yorkshire Post*, 2nd December 1922, in previewing the match, did not make the same mistake as its rival in ignoring Batley's hard won reputation in cup-ties, and mused that it was this which, if anything, would give Batley the edge over York. In the event, it was the *Leeds Mercury*'s prediction which proved to be accurate, as York won the Final by five points to nil. The *Hull Daily Mail*, 4th December 1922, characterised the game as follows:

As a dour and exciting struggle of the old-fashioned Yorkshire Cup-tie character, Saturday's game was well worthy of the big attendance. York won essentially through their superior scrimmaging and their resolute tackling, which proved an effective see-off to Batley's faster and more polished back play.

Thus it seems that, in terms of strategy, the tables were turned on Batley. The past masters of defensive rugby had been hoist by their own petard. No matter, it would not be long before the "Gallant Youths" could celebrate the acquisition of not one, but two trophies in the same season. Batley's Boxing Day match against Dewsbury at Mount Pleasant in 1922 attracted a crowd of 15,000, a clear indication that the team still had some pulling power, and large though it was it would be eclipsed three years later in a cup-tie against Leeds. Batley also continued to confound those who, from earlier times, associated the club with an unadventurous approach to the game, as may be seen from the following comment in the *Hull Daily Mail*, 30th December 1922, in its preview of Hull's home fixture against Batley: "The "Gallant Youths" are one of the three teams to have beaten Hull this season, and they did this by 13-3.... The visitors have the name for playing the most attractive style of football in the League."

The report of this match in the *Hull Daily Mail*, 1st January 1923, refers to Batley as the "Blues" on account of the fact that the team wore blue jerseys, which must have been the away strip at that time. Batley lost the match by a single point, ten points to nine, but the *Hull Daily Mail* was generous in its praise of the "Gallant Youths": "The game was the most severe seen at the Boulevard this season. Kilbey, five minutes from the end scored the best try of the match after running from the half-way line .... In spite of their one point arrears, Batley were the better side, and on the run of play deserved to win."

The same newspaper, 19th January 1923, provided a very positive assessment of the Batley outfit as it looked forward to the upcoming fixture between Hull KR and Batley: "The visit of the clever Batley team tomorrow should prove one of the most attractive matches on Rovers' card. The Mount Pleasant team are one of the cleverest in the League, and judged from their exhibition at the Boulevard on New Year's Day, they certainly occupy a false position, Batley's real place on the merits of their play being much nearer the top. Should the "Gallant Youths" happen to be in that sparkling mood which made hacks of the Leeds team in the Yorkshire Cup semi-final, the homesters can look out for trouble."

As it happened, this contest did not live up to expectations, as Batley were soundly beaten by twenty points to two. It was, perhaps, this inconsistency that was, at this juncture, preventing Batley from being a serious challenger for the League Championship title. Batley's hope of Challenge Cup glory, always high given the club's history, was extinguished in February 1923 following a replay against Oldham. By all accounts the "Gallant Youths", severely discomfited by the conditions, made far too many handling errors the result of which was that they were unable to profit from a number of scoring opportunities, losing the game by fourteen points to nil. A point of interest is that the replay took place only two days after the initial game, allowing no time for any players who had incurred minor injuries to fully recover. That having been said, this pressure was nothing as compared to that which was experienced during the Easter programme of matches in 1923. Between Good Friday and Easter Tuesday the team played four matches, with many of the same players appearing in all four fixtures. It is no wonder, given that the men also had jobs, that Batley lost three and drew one of these four matches

Though Batley had consolidated its team 1922-1923, that season had been a relatively disappointing one, particularly with regard to expectations. As indicated previously, it was inconsistency of performance which had hampered the team. At one moment they could beat Leeds 28-0, or Hull KR 15-3 whilst subsequently losing to the latter by twenty four points to two. Nevertheless, in August 1923 interest in the upcoming season was intense, as indicated by a report in the *Yorkshire Evening Post*, 18th August 1923: "7,000 spectators. Some very promising local talent was on view, and one of the players on trial, Demaine, the Buslingthorpe Vale hooker, did so well that he was signed on."

The *Leeds Mercury*, 8th October 1923, reporting on Batley's 13-9 victory against Wigan, was in no doubt that the "Gallant Youths" were strong contenders for some silverware:

Batley are promising to be one of the big sides of the season. The way in which they overthrew Wigan, in the presence of 12,000, stamped them as a force to be reckoned with.

Playing delightful and open football in the first half, they beat Wigan at their own game, and within half an hour of the start they had put on thirteen points with three brilliant tries, and a couple of goals....

A more thrilling game has not been seen at Mount Pleasant for some time, a tremendous pace to the end.

The same newspaper, 5th November 1923, was equally positive, under the sub-heading "Halifax humbled at Thrum Hall", about the team's defeat of Halifax by ten points to three. According to the *Leeds Mercury,* Batley's victory, in wretched weather conditions, was built on the basis of a very sound defence and a pragmatic approach to attack. Two days later, 7th November 1923, the above journal contained a letter from a somewhat disgruntled Batley supporter who felt that 'Yorkist', a columnist in the paper, was underestimating Batley's potential to finish top of the League. Apparently, 'Yorkist', whilst congratulating Batley on their recent victories, had expressed doubts about the team's ability to sustain this level of performance. The Batley supporter thought that:

This gives those who do not watch the "Gallant Youths" play the impression that it is more by good luck than management that they have got there. Let me remind 'Yorkist' that the capacity of the men that has brought them to the proud position of leaders can keep them there, barring accidents That capacity is good, sound, and intelligent football. I would also remind 'Yorkist' his remarks are not made simply for the Leeds public but for sport-loving Englishmen as a whole, and that Leeds does not possess all the brilliant footballers.....

The editor of the *Leeds Mercury* replied to the letter, rejecting the suggestion of pro-Leeds bias in the paper, and though the whole exchange was conducted in a civilised manner, it is hard to avoid the sense of resentment felt by the spectator from the smaller town against its big city neighbour. In November 1923 there was the prospect of the Yorkshire Cup Final being a Heavy Woollen Final as both Batley and Dewsbury reached the semi-finals of the Yorkshire Cup. However, this prospect evaporated when both teams lost their semi-final ties, Batley to Huddersfield by ten points to nine and Dewsbury to Hull by twelve points to three.

Yorkshire League Champions and Championship Winners
Batley finished the 1923-1924 season second in the League table, but as the top Yorkshire club they were crowned Yorkshire League Champions. Batley had won twenty five and drawn three of their thirty six league fixtures, scoring twenty points or more in eight of those matches. Fred Carter, Davidge, Murray, Rees and Williams each scored fifteen tries or more. All that remained now was for Batley to win the League Championship via the top four play-off competition, in which they faced Oldham, who had finished fourth, in the

semi-final. Batley demolished their opponents by thirty eight points to nil, scoring eight tries in the process, with Harry Rees clocking up seventeen points on his own account. Oldham, it seems were overwhelmed, and even the *Athletic News*, 28th April 1924, a Manchester-based paper, described their performance as dismal and mused that if Batley's finishing had been more ruthless Oldham would truly have been put to the sword. The Batley newspaper, *The Reporter*, 3rd May 1924, commented on what it considered to be an anti-Batley bias discernible in other newspapers:

Somehow or other, whenever Batley do an outstandingly big performance, some of the critics seem to take a delight in depreciating it, either by emphasising the weakness of the opposition , or in some other way detracting from its merit. One can imagine what would have been written by some of those critics if certain other teams had routed Oldham to a similar extent. I venture to think that we should have heard rather less about the impotence of Oldham and a good deal more about the greatness of the victors.

Consequently, the *Reporter* sought to redress the balance in its overall summary of Batley's performance: "Whatever may be said as to the character of the opposition, it cannot be denied that during the second half Batley played wonderful football. For ten or fifteen minutes in particular, the combination of the side was absolutely brilliant, the team demonstrating in unmistakeable fashion their ability to play the very best standard of Rugby football. It was a quality of football that I believe would have beaten any team in the league, and which, if it can be repeated this weekend, will, I think, ensure them the Championship."

The *Reporter* also contained a brief article about the formal presentation of the Yorkshire League Cup to Batley by

Mr. J. Wood, the chairman of the Rugby League Management Committee. Mr. Wood was full of praise for Batley, saying that throughout the season the team had played "good, sound, consistent, vigorous, yet clean football." Mr. Wood was also confident that Batley could go on to win the League Championship, though he added that, as he was supposed to be impartial, he could not say that he hoped that Batley would win the Championship! The scene was set for the showdown against Wigan at Broughton, 3rd May 1924. It is true that, as a consequence of the tour to Australasia, Wigan had five first team members missing from their squad, but Batley, for the same reason, were also without their inspirational captain, Frank Gallagher. The *Hull Daily Mail*, 5th May 1924, observed that it was not since the 1914-1915 season that the team finishing top of the League had won the Championship final, so Batley's victory by thirteen points to seven was in no way anomalous. The newspaper was clear that Batley were very worthy winners of the trophy:

No one can say that the honour which has gone to Batley is an empty one, however. As winners of the Yorkshire Championship, the Gallant Youths have had something of a record season, and the success they warranted on the play on Saturday has not reached Mount Pleasant out of its turn....

They played with an assurance and a liveliness that kept the Central Park team unbalanced to the end .... There is no doubt that they were the faster, quicker and more capable team.

As might be expected, the local newspaper, the *Reporter*, 10th May 1924, contained a very lengthy article celebrating Batley's achievement. The Championship trophy was the only trophy that Batley had not yet won, so the victory was all the sweeter. "Sportsman", writing his column in the

Reporter, was clear in his view that what Batley achieved 1923-1924 eclipsed anything which had gone before:

Great as have been the achievements of the past, the season just concluded stands out as the most brilliant in the long and honourable history of the club. Personally, I have always regarded the championship of the Rugby League as a very much greater honour than the winning of the challenge cup. After all, the latter only involves success in about half-a-dozen matches in which the luck of the draw and other elements of fortune not infrequently play an important part, whereas the championship of the League reflects sustained effort throughout the whole of the season against the best clubs in the game.

"Sportsman" may very well have been right that winning the League Championship was a more substantial achievement than winning the Challenge Cup, but Batley's legendary status in the history of Rugby League derives from its Challenge Cup victories, not from its Championship triumph, commendable though that was. Nevertheless, "Sportsman" was keen to debunk any notion that Batley only won because Wigan had to field a weakened team:

And Whilst everybody must have feelings of sympathy with Wigan in the absence of five prominent men in the final, I think it is stretching the thing too far to suggest that Batley would not have had any chance of success if the Wigan tourists had been available for Saturday's match. Wigan had reserves for whom most teams would be very glad to find a place in their first teams; yet Batley showed such marked superiority in the game that there is no sort of justification for the imputation that against the "real Wigan" they would have had no chance of success.

World War One and its Aftermath

Obviously, Batley's task would have been more difficult if Wigan had been able to field a full strength team, but it must be remembered that Batley had defeated Wigan earlier in the season, albeit at Mount Pleasant, by thirteen points to nine. The general consensus was that Batley were worthy Champions. The *Batley News*, 10th May 1924, included extensive coverage of the victory celebrations and the civic reception which took place when the team returned to Batley with the trophy. As in the past, the streets were lined with well-wishers as the players were transported by motor coach from the railway station to the Town Hall. Interestingly, Mr. J. Whitaker, chairman of Batley C.A. and F.C, drew particular attention to the importance of the club in regard to the town's image, highlighting the fact that Batley was as well known for football as it was for its economic activity. Following the official reception in the Town Hall, the team continued their procession around the town, the coaches drawing to a halt outside the Commercial Hotel, Clerk Green, of which the licensee was one Frank Gallagher, so that three cheers could be given for the Batley captain who was on his way to Australasia. No doubt those cheers were very loud, and they needed to be in order to resonate throughout the long years until Batley next won a trophy.

However, Batley were not quite done yet. The following season was a reasonably successful one with regard to the League, Batley winning twenty out of thirty six league games. At the start of the season, Cyril Stacey, who had been recruited from Halifax, was struck on the head by a stone thrown from the crowd during a game against Keighley at Lawkholme Lane on 6th September 1924. Stacey, having been sent off, was leaving the field when the missile was launched from the crowd. The perpetrator was apprehended by some Batley fans who promptly handed him over to the police. The

Batley News, 13th September 1924, reported that the miscreant had been prosecuted, found guilty and fined £3. In his defence, he had claimed that he had only thrown one" clinker"!

One of the most keenly fought matches was the game against Oldham, 15th November 1924, which Batley won by eleven points to seven. Both teams had reached the final of their respective County Cup Competitions, so they were evenly matched, the result of which was a ding-dong game in front of almost ten thousand spectators. The *Leeds Mercury*, 17th November 1924, recorded that:

Collectively, the Batley backs were a more effective combination than Oldham, and if they had had the ball from the scrimmages more it is probable their victory would have been more decisive....

Although the Batley forwards were not too successful in the scrimmages, two or three of them were magnificent in the open. Fred Carter, the ex-Leeds man, played one of his big games as loose-forward, whilst Jack Smith and George Douglas were again in great form.

A Record Crowd

Batley lost the Yorkshire Cup Final against Wakefield by the narrowest of margins, eight points to nine and then in March 1925 they faced Leeds in the third round of the Challenge Cup, having beaten Swinton and Widnes in the previous rounds. Batley lost this tie as well, by four points to five, but the crowd at this game numbered almost 24,000 spectators. To those readers who may have attended the cup-tie against Hunslet in 1964, when there was a crowd of approximately 14,000 packed in to Mount Pleasant, the prospect of an additional ten thousand people in the stadium is almost impossible to contemplate. That there was no serious crush within the crowd is equally remarkable. The official attendance was registered as 23,982 and by all accounts Batley were unlucky to lose, Leeds securing their victory with a converted try that many of those present thought should have been disallowed for a knock-on. Such was the interest and excitement generated by the fixture, the local magistrates, in an uncharacteristic move, had agreed to allow fifteen pubs to open half an hour earlier. Apparently the local magistrates had a well-known reputation for refusing such requests, and according to the *Reporter*, 21st March 1925, one Batley supporter jokingly suggested that Batley had lost because the players were still in shock from the magistrates' decision. Of course, the half-hour extension to drinking hours did not lead, as some temperance advocates had predicted, to rampant drunkenness. *The Reporter* noted that:

Of the conduct of their customers, licensees speak in the highest terms of praise. There was practically no trouble, they say, and people were most orderly. "Can I give any reason for this?" said one publican. "Of course I can. People did not come in to drink, but to have a snack, and after they were served it was only a few minutes before they were off. There was no drinking for the sake of drinking."

In fact the decision to allow the pubs an extra half-hour was eminently sensible and boosted the profit of those local hostelries which had the foresight to stock up on pies and sandwiches. The club had, by the mid-1920s, reached the pinnacle of its success, both in terms of trophies and spectator numbers. What followed was a definite trough, both with regard to performances on the field and the club's financial affairs.

What Goes Up: 1925-30

During the period August 1925 to April 1930 Batley played 186 league fixtures, of which they won 67 and drew nine. The most successful season was 1925-1926, during which they won 20 of their 38 league fixtures, whilst the least successful was the season 1929-30, during which they won only 7 of their 36 league matches. Also, for a club famed for its cup-fighting spirit and experience, Batley's performance in both the Yorkshire Cup and Challenge Cup Competitions during this period was equally dismal. On only two occasions did the team progress to the third round of the Challenge Cup, whilst on three occasions they were eliminated from the Yorkshire Cup in the first round. All of this serves to illustrate the difficulty of sustaining success, the lack of which can very quickly lead to a downward spiral. This is precisely what appears to have happened at Batley. During Batley's triumphant season 1923-1924 only eight players made their debuts, but there were no fewer than twenty six players who made debut appearances 1929-1930, whilst twenty four players had appeared for the first time during the previous season. In these circumstances it is difficult to maintain consistent performances and the club, as it had done in the early 1900s, became one of the also-rans.

Of course, this period was not one of unremitting gloom and though attendances declined some fixtures were still able to excite interest, particularly during the Christmas break. The *Yorkshire Post*, 24th December 1925, contained a notice about trains that were to run on Christmas Day from Leeds Central Station to Batley for spectators who wished to attend the Batley v Leeds match. It is quite remarkable by modern standards that trains were running on Christmas Day and also that matches were scheduled to take place. Usually the fixtures commenced at either 11.00am or midday so that both spectators and players could return home to enjoy their Christmas dinner. The highlight of the following season was undoubtedly the victory by nineteen points to seventeen over the New Zealand tourists in November 1926. This was also the year in which The Batley Supporters' Club was founded, the activities of which will feature more prominently in subsequent decades. Spirits at the club were lifted in January 1927 by the signing of Joe Oliver. The *Yorkshire Post and Leeds Intelligencer*, 26th January 1927, recorded the event: "As a set-off against the placing of Harry Rees and W. R. Smith on the transfer list, Batley directors yesterday morning signed on Joe Oliver, the Cumberland and former Huddersfield full-back and centre three-quarter, at a fee of £350."

Oliver was a very useful acquisition for the "Gallant Youths", but his presence alone could not arrest the decline in performance. He was selected to play for England against Wales in early January 1928, in which respect he was not dissimilar to Norman Field who was selected to play for Great Britain whilst playing for Batley in the early 1960s. Both men were outstanding players who were able to rise above the fortunes of a struggling team. Batley's performances on the field were reflected in the rapid fall in attendances at Mount Pleasant. The *Yorkshire Post*, 28th March 1927, reported that barely 2,000 spectators had watched Batley's home game against Oldham, from which, given the substance of the report, they probably returned home dissatisfied: "Oldham had first use of the slope and breeze, but both sides showed a lamentable lack of enterprise and attempts to score were of the weakest possible character."

The same newspaper, 11th April 1927, noted that fewer than 2,000 spectators had attended last Saturday's game between Batley and Wakefield at Mount Pleasant. This was only two years on from the record crowd of almost 24,000, powerful evidence that what goes up can very quickly come down. The furthest Batley progressed in any Cup competition was the third round of the Challenge Cup, which they reached in 1927 and 1928. In 1928 they came closest to progressing to the quarter finals, losing to Hull by six points to two in the second replay, the first two games having ended as 0-0 draws.

Financial Affairs

The first publication of an official match programme for home games took place on 4th September 1920, a means of keeping fans abreast of developments at the club and of making a small profit from advertising revenue. The *Yorkshire Post*, 23rd March 1922, recorded that Batley C.A. and F.C. was, at last, to become a Limited Liability Company. As noted in a previous chapter, this move was first attempted in 1899 followed by several abortive attempts in the intervening years, but this time, as reported in the *Yorkshire Post*, the precise terms were agreed:

At a special meeting of the members of the Batley Cricket, Athletic and Football Club last night, it was decided that the club should be a Limited Liability Company , with a capital of £5,000, comprising 5,000 shares of £1 each. The scheme as approved, provides that no person shall hold more than fifty shares, that no person with less than two £1 shares shall have voting rights, that the qualification for the directorate shall be the holding of 25 shares, that the number of directors shall be nine, that the company shall guarantee an annual dividend of 2.5% on shares, and should it be unable to pay that dividend the directors shall be personally responsible for paying that dividend.

World War One and its Aftermath

The *Leeds Mercury*, 24th May 1924, reported that Batley's finances were healthy, with a profit of £217 for the past year in spite of the fact that the cricket section of the club along with the reserve football team had incurred substantial losses. Though the cricket team had won both the Heavy Woollen Challenge Cup and the Heavy Woollen League in 1922, it had to be subsidised by the even more successful rugby football team, whilst the reserve squad was probably thought of as a loss leader. The *Yorkshire Post*, 9th May 1925, noted that Batley C.A and F.C had finished the financial year with a profit of £257 and a balance in hand and at the bank of £1,004. The football 'gate' receipts amounted to £10,466, a record for the club and a sum which was equivalent to £598,486 in 2017. Of course, £1,693 had been taken at one single game, the cup-tie against Leeds in March 1925. The club had also spent £524 on improvements and repairs to the ground, a substantial chunk of which may have been used to repair the roof of the stand which had, as reported in the *Leeds Mercury*, 3rd January 1925, been damaged by a gale-force wind: "A considerable portion of the roof of the covered stand on the Mount Pleasant football ground was blown clean from its position into the middle of the field."

This reasonably comfortable financial position had been achieved on the back of two very successful years for the club, but even so not all of the shareholders were satisfied, one of the perils of the club having become a Limited Liability Company. The *Yorkshire Post*, 14th May 1925, reported that some shareholders, unhappy with the amount of money that was in the reserve fund, had accused the directors of extravagance. Little did they know that by the end of the decade the club's finances would be in a much worse condition.

The General Strike took place in May 1926, but many

miners continued to resist until November of that year when they were forced to return to work on the mine owners' terms by what the renowned historian A. J. P. Taylor described as "the lash of hunger." The economic conditions which prevailed in Britain during the late 1920s, in part caused by a return to the gold standard, disproportionately affected the industrial areas in which rugby league was king, as was the case following the financial crash of 2008. As a consequence 'gate' receipts were bound to suffer. Fans may have wished to relieve the monotony and misery of unemployment by attendance at a match, but they had to have the wherewithal to pay the entrance fee. The *Hull Daily Mail*, 30th August 1926, reported the following:

About two thousand mine workers besieged the gates at Featherstone Rovers versus Batley Rugby League match at Featherstone on Saturday, and demanded admission free. The home club authorities were in a quandary, for the men refused to go away and the consent of the visiting club, who take 10% of the receipts, was eventually obtained, and the crowd were allowed free entrance.

By the end of the decade poor performances on the field coupled with increasing levels of unemployment combined to create acute financial difficulties for Batley C.A. and F.C. The club had to sell its star player, Joe Oliver, in the early part of the 1928-1929 season in order to generate some hard cash, establishing a pattern that would be repeated in subsequent years with players such as Bill Hudson, John Etty, Tommy Martyn and Carl Gibson, as the club found it impossible to hang on to its top class players. The *Leeds Mercury*, 20th February 1929, outlined the potential gravity of Batley's situation whilst also seeking to reassure fans.

World War One and its Aftermath

That the present position of the club and its immediate prospects are none too rosy cannot be denied .... it is understood that the club is losing a considerable amount of money on the present season's working , and the probability is that the financial position will be worse rather than better by the end of the season....

Obviously, therefore, the present position of the directors is a difficult one, but any idea that the club, with its magnificent record of past achievements will be allowed to go out of existence may be at once dispelled.

The *Yorkshire Evening Post*, 28th February 1929 and the *Sheffield Daily Independent*, 1st March 1929, both emphasised the extent to which Batley's 'gate' receipts had been badly affected by the economic downturn of the past few years, a stark example of which was the fact that at the end of the 1928-1929 season the 'gate' receipts only amounted to £2,561 as compared with an average of £10,000 in the period 1919-1925, as reported in the *Yorkshire Evening Post*, 8th May 1929, which also noted that the present board of nine directors was not seeking re-election at the upcoming annual meeting. The *Leeds Mercury*, 15th June 1929, under the heading "Batley's Forward Policy," drew attention to a statement issued by the new board of directors at the club:

Recognising the need for new blood in the football team, the directors point out that football is essentially a young man's game, and without implying any disloyalty to old players, they declare that when a servant of the club is unable to reach the required standard, he must be replaced. Emphasising the importance of team spirit, the directors state that to encourage its development, they have decided to give the same rate of pay to all members of the team.

Of course, as they looked to the future, Batley's directors were grappling with the perennial issues that face all clubs: when to dispense with ageing players and how much to pay members of the team. Unfortunately for Batley, and for all other rugby league clubs, the economic future was about to get a whole lot worse as the effects of the Wall Street Crash began to be felt in the subsequent decade.

Charity Matches at Mount Pleasant

The staging of charity matches, both for local causes and sometimes for past players became something of a tradition at Batley C.A.and F.C. The *Hull Daily Mail*, 9th February 1921, recorded that 4,000 spectators had attended a match at Mount Pleasant between the present Batley team and a team of 'stars' for the joint benefit of three former Batley forwards, Fred Hill, Harry Hodgson and Arthur Kitson. The first two beneficiaries had turned out for the 'stars' alongside such luminaries as Billy Batten, Jonty Parkin and Joe Lyman. In September 1922 the local Licensed Victuallers Association organised a Wednesday afternoon charity match, attended by 2,000 spectators, for the benefit of the Batley and District Hospital which received about £100. In the days before the establishment of the NHS, this money was absolutely vital for local hospitals, so it is no surprise to read a report in the *Yorkshire Post*, 4th May 1925, about a charity match at Mount Pleasant, organised by members of the rag trade in the Heavy Woollen District in aid of Dewsbury Infirmary and Batley Hospital. According to the newspaper:

Prior to the game £250 had been raised by a subscription list limited to members and the trade, and about 1,000 people attended the game between teams of "raggers" representing Batley, Morley and District, and Dewsbury, Ossett and District. Mr. J.W. Fox and Mr. W.J. Ineson, respective presidents of the Infirmary and Hospital took the forward kick-off, and in an entertaining game the Batley-Morley team won by 2 goals to 1 goal.

Perhaps the most interesting charity match which took place at Mount Pleasant in the 1920s and one which became an annual event, was the Veterans v Police, the proceeds of which were donated to the Northern Police Orphanage, Batley Hospital and Batley Ambulance. The *Batley News*, 24th April 1926, described how one such match was refereed by Wilfred Auty, with the support of Herbert Simms and Mark Shackleton as touch judges. Former Batley players 'Wattie' Davies, Jack Etty, Jack Goodall, Jim Gath and Herbert Goosey turned out for the veterans in a game which, according to the *Batley News*: "....was much more seriously contested than many people imagined it would be." And in which: "Some of the veterans gave glimpses of their old skill and craftiness. Jack Goodall showed that he still knows how to cut through and hand off, whilst Jim Gath led the front line in his old style, and the Veterans forwards were to the fore in gaining possession from the scrummages."

Rugby Union in Batley in the 1920s

Though the Batley Rugby Union Club had been disbanded in 1914, having subsequently been reformed, it was active during the 1920s. The *Leeds Mercury*, 14th December 1922, makes direct reference to the Batley Rugby Union Club's fixture against Yarnbury RUFC (Horsforth). However, the prospect of any rapprochement between the two codes was extremely unlikely, a stark reminder of which may be seen in the Rugby Union's rules relating to professionalism, as noted in the *Yorkshire Post*, 26th February 1923:

An act of professionalism is:- Playing on any ground where gate money is taken in any match or contest where it is agreed that less than fifteen players on each side shall take part.

Knowingly playing with or against any suspended player or club, or with or against any professional player or club.

Presumably, rugby union 'sevens' tournaments had not yet been developed. A clear difference between the two codes, and one which became even sharper later in the century, was the presence of professionally qualified men within the ranks of rugby union teams.

The *Leeds Mercury*, 1st March 1924, in previewing Batley Rugby Union Club's fixture against Otley, lists Dr. F.A. Smorfitt as a member of the Batley team. Whilst the "Gallant Youths" prospered in the early 1920s, the Batley RUFC was sufficiently vibrant to be able to field a reserve team. The *Sports Special Green 'Un*, 8th November 1924, refers to a Batley RUC reserve team fixture against Barnsley 'A' team. Furthermore, the *Yorkshire Evening Post*, 23rd January 1926, refers to the possibility that S.R. Whitfield, the Batley RUFC forward, might be selected to play for England against Ireland.

However, the local rugby union club, like its league counterpart, experienced financial difficulties during this decade, as noted in the *Leeds Mercury*, 17th June 1926, which recorded that Batley RUFC had made a loss of £49 during the past year. The *Yorkshire Post and Leeds Intelligencer*, 9th January 1928, included reports of matches played by Batley C.A. and F.C and Batley RUFC in the same edition. However, during this period there is no clear evidence of any cross fertilisation between the two clubs, and, given the draconian rules of the Rugby Union, that is hardly surprising.

World War One and its Aftermath

Off the field Shenanigans and tragic events

As in previous decades some individuals associated with Batley C.A. and F.C. fell foul of the law and ended up in court. The *Yorkshire Evening Post*, 2nd January 1920, under the heading "Batley Footballer Protests His Innocence", reported that: "Thomas Brannan, the Batley footballer, was charged at Batley, today, with having been drunk and riotous in New Street, at 11.35pm, on Boxing Day Night."

'Dowdy' pleaded not guilty, saying that he had been teetotal since the previous July, but added that if he was going to end up in court anyway, he might as well take up drinking again! Having been found guilty, and with five previous convictions on record, he was offered the choice of paying a fine of thirty shillings or spending sixteen days in prison. He chose the latter. The same newspaper, 20th January 1920, contained a fairly lengthy story about the prosecution, for assault, of the Batley player, Thomas Murphy. According to the prosecution Murphy had assaulted Miss Emily Hemingway, a woman with whom he had been having an affair, on several occasions. She had gone to stay with an aunt in Normanton in order to avoid Murphy's attention, but on her return Murphy confronted her in Batley Market Place.

The prosecuting lawyer, as reported in the *Yorkshire Evening Post*, said: "She would have nothing to do with him, but he followed her, picked her up and carried her about. Then he kicked her, leaving her in a deplorable condition. She went to the police-station and an inspector saw her state. He (Murphy) afterwards sent a letter of apology to her, blaming being mad-drunk."

Murphy was fined 27 shillings and bound over in the sum of £5 not to molest the girl for three months, a somewhat lenient punishment by modern standards since it implies that if he assaulted Miss Hemingway after four months, he would not forfeit the £5 bond! Between 1916 and 1929 three individuals associated with the club were found guilty of violating the licensing laws. The *Leeds Mercury*, 25th January 1916, reported that Jack Rogers, the former Batley player, now the landlord of the West End Hotel, Batley, had been found guilty of serving alcohol outside of permitted hours. Of course, more restrictive licensing laws had been brought in by the Defence of the Realm Act (DORA) in 1914 and Rogers was fined 10 shillings. Similarly, both Frank Gallagher in 1927 and Jack Leeming in 1929 were fined for the same offence. According to the *Leeds Mercury*, 22nd March 1927, Frank Gallagher, the landlord of the Commercial Hotel, Clerk Green, Batley, on whose premises two men were caught drinking at 4.00pm on 27th February, stated that he had: "....called 'time' at half-past two, the regular closing time for the district, and collected most of the glasses, but not all ..... left the company of men in the snug, talking about football and went to lunch, had a bath, and completely overlooked the glasses."

In a rather different vein, with regard to off the field activities, Herbert Goosey who made his debut for Batley in January 1921, having signed for Batley from Northampton RUFC, combined his rugby career with a part-time career in boxing. He fought a bout on the night before he played for Batley against Bramley on 29th October 1921.

Batley C.A. and F.C. was also linked, in one way or another, with a number of tragic events that occurred during this period. The *Leeds Mercury*, 2nd February 1916, reported the following: "A tragic discovery was made in the football grounds at Mount Pleasant, Batley, yesterday, when the body of Miriam Thompson, 56, a widow, of Liberty Terrace, Batley, was found hanging by a large handkerchief from a beam near the boys' entrance to the field."

World War One and its Aftermath

Unfortunately, this was not the first time that Batley's ground had been the chosen location for a suicide. Sadly, the *Driffield Times*, 8th November 1919, reported the tragic death in a pit accident of the former Batley stalwart, Fred Bennett, who had commenced playing for the club in the 1880s. According to the newspaper, whilst working at Soothill Colliery: "Bennett was killed by a fall of roof whilst helping another man to finish his work. It is particularly sad to recall that about a year ago his son, Walter Bennett, lost his life in the same colliery in the same manner."

Rather closer to home in December 1921, a Keighley player, Pat Collins, died on the pitch at Mount Pleasant. Having sat on a bench at the side of the pitch, he collapsed and was dead by the time a doctor, who was present at the ground, was able to reach him. The *Yorkshire Evening Post*, 5th December 1921, reported that a post-mortem examination of Mr. Collins resulted in the conclusion that: "The cause of death was syncope, due to fibrous degeneration of the liver and spleen, accelerated by over-exertion."

It seems that Pat Collins was somewhat overweight and not as fit as he should have been. The *Sheffield Daily Telegraph*, 7th August 1923, reported the tragic death of Sam Moss, the father of the young Batley player Ernest Moss, in an accident at a level crossing in Featherstone. Apparently, Mr Moss, who was profoundly deaf, having failed to hear the train driver's whistle, had been knocked down by the train. The following year, Herbert Marsden, the Secretary of Batley C.A. and F.C, never having recovered from gas poisoning during WW1, died at the age of 30.

Perhaps the most poignant tragedy was that which befell Willie Scott, Batley's former half-back. According to the *Leeds Mercury*, 13th February 1928, on Friday 10th February: "Scott travelled by tramcar about 11.00pm, alighting at

Grafton Street, on Bradford Road from which spot he would reach Warwick Road where he lodged. After alighting he seems to have gone round the back of the car to cross Bradford Road into Grafton Street. About the same time a motor car was coming along Bradford Road in the direction of Batley. A little later Scott was found lying in the Road and died before reaching the local hospital."

The inquest into Willie Scott's death recorded a verdict of death by misadventure, concluding that he had probably slipped and fallen under the wheels of vehicle he had not seen as he emerged from behind the tram. After the inquest Willie Scott's body was transported back to Jedburgh, where his funeral took place. In a fitting tribute to the deceased, for some distance along Bradford Road a large procession escorted the vehicle transporting his body back to Scotland.

World War One and its Aftermath

TIMELINE: THE 1930s
UK and World Events

1930 – The first FIFA World Cup Tournament is held in
Uruguay
The YHA opens its first youth hostel
1931 – The Highway Code is issued for the first time
The Empire State Building is completed
1932 – The mass trespass on Kinder Scout
The first Mars bar is produced, in Slough
1933 – The National Grid is completed in Great Britain
Prohibition ends in the USA
1934 – The Night of the Long Knives in Nazi Germany
The liner, The Queen Mary is launched
1935 – The driving test becomes compulsory in the UK
Mussolini invades Abyssinia
1936 – The Spanish Civil War begins
Edward VIII abdicates
1937 – The coronation of George VI and Queen Elizabeth
Japan invades China
1938 – Austria votes to unite with Germany
Neville Chamberlain signs the Munich Agreement
with Hitler
1939 – The Spanish Civil War ends in victory for Franco
UK declares war on Nazi Germany

6

THE HUNGRY THIRTIES: 1930-1940

Following the successes of the 1920s, the next decade marked the beginning of a very long barren period, which lasted until 1998, during which Batley RLFC won no trophies at all. That is not to say that for seventy three years Batley produced neither star players nor teams capable of competing with the best, rather it was that the vital ingredients of skill and consistency were never present in the right combination for long enough. During the 1930s the club was hungry for success, success that was not forthcoming. Of course, in addition to this metaphorical hunger there was also literal hunger in the town as a consequence of the Depression. The *Yorkshire Post*, 27th December 1932, reporting on the derby game against Dewsbury at Mount Pleasant on Boxing Day, noted that: "The game was witnessed by 8,000 people, including 800 wholly unemployed, who were admitted on payment of sixpence and the production of their National Health Insurance cards...."

During the Depression sport was, along with the cinema, one of main diversions from the grinding hardship and poverty of this period. However, for the Batley fans the 1930s offered little that could lift their spirits. In the 1929-1930 season Batley won only seven of their thirty six league matches, finishing second from bottom of the table. The following two seasons during which they won, respectively, twelve and sixteen matches from thirty eight in each season, provided minor respite from the earlier gloom. 1932-1933 the tally was thirteen wins from thirty eight fixtures followed by a slight improvement 1933-1934 during which there were sixteen victories from thirty eight league matches. The worst season was 1934-1935 which saw Batley win only nine of their thirty eight league fixtures. The team did not register a victory until the 13th October 1934 when they beat Dewsbury by six points to nil. The best performance in the league came in the following season, 1935-1936, with eighteen wins from thirty eight games, before a relapse in the following season during which they won only twelve of their thirty eight matches. The 1937-1938 season was the most successful overall. Though the team fell one short of their tally of victories in 1935-1936, with seventeen wins from thirty eight league games, Batley progressed to both the semi-final of the Yorkshire Cup and the third round of the Challenge Cup during this season. With regard to the Cup Competitions, the previous seasons had been a sorry tale of early exits for the once formidable cup fighting club. In 1938-1939, the last season before the commencement of the Second World War, Batley managed only eleven victories from forty league fixtures, suffering seven straight losses at the end of the season.

Though the overall performance of the team was, at best, mediocre during this decade, some significant players made their debuts for Batley during the 1930s: George Goldie, August 1932 (141 appearances); Mick Foley, October 1933 (236); F. T. Adams, November 1933 (34); Ivor Frowen, December 1933 (93); George Brown, April 1935 (258 apps, 418 goals); Bill Hudson, August 1935 (207); Don Pollard, August 1935 (117); Dicky Ralph, August 1937 (45). Though Adams and Ralph each played fewer than fifty games for the 'Gallant Youths', their respective stars shone very brightly whilst they were members of the Batley team. The *Leeds Mercury*, 23rd July 1932 and 28th August 1937, recorded the transfers of Goldie and Ralph from Leeds to Batley, in each case singing the praises of the respective players, describing the latter as the best stand-off to come from Welsh Rugby Union. Similarly, the *Hull Daily Mail*, 29th November 1933, noted that Batley had made an astute move in capturing both F.T. Adams and Ivor Frowen from Halifax.

A Decade without Success
From the outset it seems that the club struggled to find a winning formula, unable to establish a stable team. The *Leeds Mercury*, 18th January 1930, refers to the problems of selection faced by the Batley directors, noting that: "Throughout the season the Batley directors, their recruiting activities curbed by the thinness of their purse, have had to experiment match after match. Only two of the backs who played last week have been retained for this game, and their positions have been changed."

The same newspaper, 30th January 1930, suggested that Batley was involved in a desperate search for new recruits as a means of invigorating the team. Of course, as noted in the above extract, the principal restraint was the lack of finance. No fewer than twenty seven players made debut appearances during the 1929-1930 season, Harold V. Nunn being the only notable name. Without the ready cash it was difficult for the club to build a team that could compete with the best.

At the end of 1930 Batley encountered a problem of a different kind, one that resulted from a combination of inclement weather and the obduracy of their arch rivals, Dewsbury. The derby match between the two teams, scheduled for Boxing Day 1930, was cancelled as a result of a heavy snow fall. The game was re-scheduled for New Year's Day, 1931, but Dewsbury, with an upcoming match against Huddersfield on 3rd January, refused to play. As a consequence, Batley, eager to attract as large a crowd as possible, advertised the fixture whilst appealing to the Rugby League secretary for a ruling in their favour. The *Yorkshire Evening Post*, 30th December 1930, was quite explicit about the reasons why Batley insisted on the game being played on New Year's Day:

A Batley director told a Yorkshire Evening Post *reporter: "It is our match and we want New year's Day because £200 now is worth more to the Batley club than say £250 in March. We think that we can get £350 by playing on Thursday, because there is so much holiday making in the district and it would be the equivalent of Christmas Day or Boxing Day.*

The Dewsbury directors claimed that Batley had acted both precipitously and discourteously in cancelling the Boxing Day match, a claim that was strenuously denied by Batley, but in the end they complied with the ruling made by the Rugby League Management Committee that the game had to be played on 1st January 1931. Batley may have won the argument, but they lost the match by seven points to two in a game which, according to the *Yorkshire Post*, 2nd January 1931, was both exciting and free of foul play, a somewhat unusual occurrence for a derby game and especially for one which had been preceded by an acrimonious dispute. To rub salt into Batley's wounds, Joe Oakland's son had turned out for Dewsbury.

In September 1931, Oldham came to Mount Pleasant seeking their first victory there since 1905. The game, which

Batley won by fifteen points to nil, was played in front of a crowd of 5,000, an indication that, in spite of Batley's indifferent performances, attendances were holding up reasonably well. The main feature of the game was the sending off of four players, two from each team, though the match was not seemingly characterised by any excessive brutality. Oldham also lost a player through injury in the second half, the result of which was that the scrums were contested by only the front row of each team. The *Leeds Mercury*, 28th September 1931, was quite optimistic about Batley's prospects for the rest of the season, describing the 'Gallant Youths' as a "considerably improved side this season." The improvement turned out to be limited as Batley still won fewer than half of their league games during this season, towards the end of which the same newspaper, 29th March 1932, covering Batley's away game against Featherstone, echoed previous reports that Batley, though slightly unlucky, were not quite good enough to seal a victory.

Batley commenced the 1932-1933 season with two convincing wins, away to Featherstone by nineteen points to nine and at home to Halifax by eighteen points to five. The *Leeds Mercury*, 28th August 1932, reported that: "The Batley directors left Featherstone in a delightful mood, and they had cause for jubilation. The margin of ten points did not flatter the Batley team in the least .... Batley have two grand forwards in Walker and Earnshaw .... and a back division which should bring many victories to the club."

The *Yorkshire Post*, 5th September 1932, in its report of Batley's win against Halifax, was not quite so flattering, choosing to emphasise the unimaginative approach of Batley's backs, noting only that Batley made more effective use of the strong wind than their opponents did. In the end, it was the latter report that turned out to be more prescient as Batley were unable to sustain their promising start to the season. The *Leeds Mercury*, 9th September 1932, reporting on Batley's loss at Warrington by twenty three points to nil, suggested that the Batley players were not as fit as they should be:

Batley were no match for Warrington at Wilderspool last night. Without producing their best form, Warrington accounted for Batley with ease. In every department they were superior, and at no stage was the result in doubt. All the thrills were by the home team who stayed the pace better.

Batley appeared to be out of condition and too slow to check the running backs.

By the end of September 1932 Batley were being lambasted by the *Yorkshire Post*, 26th September 1932, for their abject performance at home to Bradford Northern, a game which Batley lost by twenty points to eight. The newspaper described both teams as equally unimpressive, but drew attention to Batley's lack of both imagination and cohesion. Ominously, the attendance at this match was only a little over 2,000, a warning that economic conditions were beginning to bite. In December 1932 Batley had high hopes that J.R Tibbs (aged 26), who had appeared as a trialist for Batley in 1924 but had since been in the army, could beef up the three-quarter line. Unfortunately, in spite of very positive reports about his performances whilst playing for the army, he never made a single appearance for the first team. At the end of February 1933 Batley's Challenge Cup tie against Warrington was postponed because of heavy snow and the re-scheduled game also had to be rearranged because conditions had not sufficiently improved. The *Yorkshire Post*, 27th February 1933, reported the following:

....the report from Batley last night was that the Mount Pleasant ground was under three to four feet of snow, that there were deep drifts on the cricket field, through which spectators cross to get to the football ground, and considerable drifts outside the ground. The snow has drifted into the stands.

This was a considerable blow to Batley because a large crowd had been expected to attend this cup clash which had been initially scheduled for Saturday 25th February, but which was eventually played on Tuesday 7th March, in front of a diminished crowd. This was revenue that the club could ill afford to lose. The story of the 1932-1933 season is summed up by Batley's performance in their final home game against Featherstone. In the last minute of the game, with the scores tied at ten points each, Batley had the chance to secure a victory, but Goldie missed a penalty kick from directly in front of the posts!

At the start of the new season. 1933-1934, as noted in the *Leeds Mercury*, 1st September 1933, there was a concerted attempt at Batley to introduce new faces into the team. The aforementioned newspaper recorded that, for their away fixture at Parkside, Batley had selected two junior players, Watson and Collier, in place of regulars, Nunn and Shirley. In the event, it was Swift who was replaced by Collier, but the experiment did not work as Batley lost the match by 21 points to thirteen. Nonetheless, the 'Gallant Youths' needed all the players they could muster and it was doubtless for this reason that Batley attempted to have the 'sine die' suspension on Eddie Donnelly lifted. However, as reported in the *Hull Daily Mail*, 13th September 1933, the Rugby League Management Committee flatly refused Donnelly's appeal for a re-hearing. The *Hull Daily Mail*, 9th November 1933, *Leeds*

Mercury, 9th November 1933 and *Batley Reporter*, 10th November 1933, all recorded Batley's acquisition of the former Dewsbury and Batley Rugby Union forward, Hartley Booth, who was also the licensee of the New Inn, Batley. Booth went on to make just over seventy appearances for the first team, kicking thirty one goals.

In November 1933, Walter Swift, Batley's half-back, suffered a serious injury in a match against Hull at the Boulevard. Swift, having crashed into boards that were used on the dog track which surrounded the football pitch, suffered a double fracture of his jaw, an injury which caused him to miss 12 matches. As a consequence, in the hope of acquiring some compensation from Hull, Batley lodged a complaint with the Rugby League Management Committee, but no money was forthcoming. The *Yorkshire Post* and *Leeds Mercury*, 5th February 1934, both covered in some detail Batley's derby game against Dewsbury, a game which Batley, despite being the favourites to win, lost by ten points to six. What is interesting about the headline in the *Leeds Mercury* ("How the Dewsbury Plans were Wrecked") is that it contradicts the bulk of the text which suggests that it was in fact Batley's plans that were stymied by their opponents. It was probably a misprint and the headline should read "How the Batley Plans Were Wrecked". Dewsbury, it seems, playing an uncomplicated style of rugby were able to pressurise Batley, whose backs lacked pace and fluidity, into making basic errors.

The *Yorkshire Post* was quite precise in its assessment of why Dewsbury were able to win the game: "Acceptance of chances, deadly tackling by backs who stood well up and seldom missed their man, and equally deadly tackling by forwards, who also gave the opposing six a lesson in how to play the ball and atoned for their failure in the scrums, were the factors giving Dewsbury the victory they deserved."

The *Leeds Mercury*, somewhat surprisingly, observed that the 6,000 'gate' was poor for a derby match, but given the economic strictures of the mid-1930s an attendance of this size was well above average. In their last match of this season, in April 1934, Batley played London Highfield in a floodlit game at the White City, west London. Batley's opponents had evolved from Wigan Highfield and subsequently became Liverpool Stanley, but for one season as London Highfield they played their home fixtures at the White City Stadium. The *Batley Reporter*, 21st April 1934, contained a detailed article about Batley's floodlit encounter in the capital, which Batley won by nine points to seven. According to the *Batley Reporter*:

One of the players likened the experience to playing in brilliant sunshine and to both players and spectators there was a real, or imaginary, sense of heat from the arc lamps used for floodlighting. Neither players nor spectators found any difficulty in following the flight of the ball, and although heavy rain fell for a time during the progress of Wednesday's game, the conditions were otherwise pleasant and enjoyable.

As indicated earlier, the 1934-1935 season was the worst of the decade for Batley as the team recorded only nine wins from thirty eight league matches. One of the few highlights of this season was Batley's victory against Swinton, at the beginning of November 1934, by nine points to seven after their opponents had chalked up nine consecutive wins. The *Leeds Mercury*, 5th November 1934, was unequivocal in claiming that Batley had secured this notable victory entirely on merit. According to the newspaper: "Batley played easily their best football of the season and they were responsible for the brightest moments in the game. As a combination the

Batley backs were superior to Swinton's and for once, the famous Swinton forwards met their match in the splendid Batley pack."

The *Yorkshire Post*, 28th January 1935, considered that, though Castleford had been the better team, Batley did not deserve to lose against them at Mount Pleasant by twenty points to nine. That having been said, Castleford did outscore Batley by six tries to three, so the *Yorkshire Post*'s suggestion that had Batley possessed a reliable goal kicker they could have run Castleford much closer, rings rather hollow given that Castleford failed with five attempted conversions. By the beginning of March 1935 Batley had lost eight consecutive matches, the most recent one being a home fixture against Oldham, at which the attendance was below 2,000, providing receipts of only £70. This was a difficult time for the club.

During the following season, in which Batley won twice as many matches as they had in 1934-1935, the team played for the first time at Acton and Willesden's Park Royal Stadium. The *Batley Reporter*, 5th October 1935, covered the visit to North West London in some detail, noting that: "....quite a number of Batley people now living in and around London turned up at Park Royal for the match, one or two of whom have been away from Batley for many years."

The newspaper reporter also waxed lyrical about the stadium: "Although not yet completed, Park Royal is already a splendidly equipped ground. Situated a little more than a mile from the famous Wembley stadium, which is clearly visible from the entrance, the ground and its buildings are planned on the most up-to-date lines, with every modern convenience and facility. Two magnificent stands – one at each side of the playing area – provide covered seating accommodation for nearly 20,000 people, about half of which is available at the price of one shilling."

As to the game itself, which Batley lost by twenty one points to fourteen, the home team seemingly had much the better of the first half and fully deserved their lead at the interval. Batley, however, staged a second half rally in which the star performer was Harold Nunn, who scored a spectacular try. Had Batley been able to perform as well throughout the match as they performed in the last quarter, they would surely have won. Towards the end of this season as Batley completed the double over Rochdale with a victory by twenty points to fourteen, the *Leeds Mercury*, 11th April 1936, was quite effusive in its praise for the 'Gallant Youths', but the reality was that during the course of the season there were too few performances which merited such positive analysis.

....Batley were not only a well-balanced side revealing initiative and aggressiveness, but at times their play was really brilliant. They always had the measure of the Hornets and never looked likely to lose command of the game. Batley revealed splendid teamwork as well as clever individual play.

Batley's form dipped once again during the following season, 1936-1937, as the team won less than a third of its league fixtures, in addition to being knocked out of the Challenge Cup, after a replay against Castleford, in the first round. This was the year in which the Rugby League Council invited members of the public to attend the draw for the first round of the Challenge Cup, a decision which had unintended, though not entirely unpredictable consequences. The draw, which was scheduled to take place at 3.00pm on the 13th January 1937, at the Grosvenor Hotel, Manchester, attracted a huge number of would-be-spectators, the consequence of which was that the draw had to be expedited as quickly as possible in order to avoid a chaotic crush.

The Hungry Thirties

The *Yorkshire Evening Post*, 17th August 1937, just prior to the opening of the new season, was clear about what Batley was most in need of in order to improve on the previous season's performances: "....the first need is for the development of a sound half-back combination, the lack of which has been Batley's failing for several seasons."

Fortunately, Batley acquired the services of Dicky Ralph, a star player who was coming towards the end of his career, but whose presence clearly inspired the 'Gallant Youths', who enjoyed their most successful season of the decade, a season in which they reached both the semi-final of the Yorkshire Cup and the third round of the Challenge Cup. The circumstances in which Batley reached the semi-final of the Yorkshire Cup in September 1937 were somewhat controversial. Their opponents in the quarter final were Keighley, and with the scores tied at seven points each Batley were awarded a penalty a few minutes before the end of the match. George Brown missed the penalty but the referee ordered that it should be retaken because one of the Keighley players had moved whilst Brown was taking the kick. Needless to say, Brown did not miss with his second attempt and Batley progressed to the semi-final. By all accounts it was Batley's ferocious tackling which kept them in the game, most especially as they had to play the whole of the second half with twelve men, the consequence of Hudson being sent off in the first minute after the interval. Sadly, Batley lost the semi-final to Leeds, at Headingley, by ten points to five, but at least some of the legendary cup fighting spirit had been temporarily revived.

In November 1937 the Batley directors were involved in a dispute with their arch-rivals, Dewsbury, about the signing of R. E. Thomas from Halifax. Dewsbury, it seems, accused Batley of poaching the player whilst the Dewsbury directors were in negotiations about Thomas's transfer to Dewsbury. The *Yorkshire Evening Post*, 19th November 1937, printed the following statement issued by the Batley directors, who vehemently denied any improper behaviour:

The Batley club very much regrets the attitude taken up by the Dewsbury club on the question of the signing of R.E. Thomas. The Batley club maintain strongly that they have always played straight and fair in any dealings with Dewsbury or any other club. The Batley club resent any suggestion of unfair dealings, and the suggestions made can only have the effect of causing friction between the two clubs.

....Batley maintain they had an equal right with Dewsbury to try and get the player. Batley acted quickly and fairly, and went through the same procedure as had been followed in football transfers in hundreds of cases.

Dewsbury had been gazumped and they didn't like it. They liked it even less when Thomas starred in Batley's victory in the Christmas Day derby at Crown Flatt in 1937. Before the commencement of the 1938-1939 season, Batley suffered a major blow when Don Pollard broke his leg whilst painting the goalposts at Mount Pleasant, the result of which was that he was out of action for the whole of the season. According to the *Hull Daily Mail*, 16th August 1938: "....while mounting a ladder which was reared up against one of the posts the post snapped at the level of the crossbar when Pollard was about fifteen feet from the ground. As the ladder was falling, Pollard jumped clear."

The injury incurred by Don Pollard is testimony to Batley's tight financial constraints and the vital importance of volunteer work, work on which the club continues to depend. As indicated above, Dicky Ralph signed for Batley in August 1937, but in February 1939, at the age of thirty one, he decided that it was time to retire. Batley, strapped for cash in 1937, had undoubtedly made a bold move in acquiring Ralph, but in the forty five matches that he played for the team he was inspirational. His absence was keenly felt in the latter part of the last season before the Second World War broke out. Nonetheless, when he made the decision to retire, it was with the full support of the Batley directors.

The *Yorkshire Evening Post*, 10th February 1939, reported the following comment from a Batley official: "There is no friction of any sort between Ralph and the directors. The Batley club have been delighted to have his services, and we shall never forget what a loyal player and a good sportsman he has been."

Financial Affairs

As may be inferred from what has already been written about Batley RLFC during the 1930s, this was a decade in which the club struggled financially. The economic climate was not conducive to an increase in 'gate' money, quite the reverse in fact. As revenue from the turnstiles declined so did the club's ability to purchase new players, the lack of which contributed to poor performances on the field, which further led to a fall in attendances at matches. Thus Batley, like some other clubs, was caught in a spiral of decline from which it was very difficult to extricate itself. In May 1930, the club's losses over the past year were estimated to be in the region of £800.The *Hull Daily Mail*, 5th July 1930, summed up the gravity of the situation with which the Batley directors were faced: "There seems to be a serious doubt about the Batley Football Club being able to weather a financial storm long enough to permit one of the oldest rugby league clubs to fulfil its fixtures next season."

However, the *Yorkshire Post*, 5th July 1930, was clearly one step ahead of the East Yorkshire publication, because it was able to report that the possibility that Batley might not be able to fulfil its fixture commitments had been averted, primarily, it seems, as a consequence of the efforts of Dr. Walker and Ernest Kirk, two former chairmen of the club. Apparently these two men had managed to raise £1,200 and had begun the process of organising a scheme for the reconstruction of club finances, coupled with the introduction of a team-building committee whose task was to obtain new players for the team. The club's anxiety about its future prospects was further heightened in August 1930 with the news that the Huddersfield Town reserve team was to play its home games at Savile Town. As the *Hull Daily Mail*, 2nd August 1930 expressed it: "'Soccer every Saturday' is not a slogan welcomed by the professional Rugby clubs in the Heavy Woollen district." Batley could ill afford to have its already declining attendances further reduced by an Association Football rival.

By May 1937 Batley RLFC was able to report that, though it still was in debt to the tune of £2,517, it had actually made a profit of £102 during the past year. The bulk of the debt was a bank overdraft of £1,980, secured by the personal guarantee of the directors and friends of the club. The *Yorkshire Evening Post*, 27th May 1937, noted that, at the annual general meeting, Batley chairman Ernest Kirk had suggested it might be an appropriate moment to launch a public appeal for funds in order to enable the club to strengthen the squad. This suggestion was taken up by the Mayor of Batley, the former player, George Main, who launched the 'Shilling Fund' in February 1938. The *Batley Reporter*, 5th February 1938, covering the event in some detail, drew attention to the fact that the club had always operated within tight financial margins, even in the heady days of the 1890s. The newspaper reported that Kirk thought that in retrospect the decision to become a limited company had been a mistake. According to the *Batley News* he said: "I know it cleared the debt and was the only way that could be thought of at the time, but we lost the members' interest to a large extent, and, to my mind, we want to get back to a members' club as soon as possible."

An account was opened at the Midland Bank in the name of 'The Mayor of Batley's Appeal Fund', and by 23rd May 1938, the *Leeds Mercury* was able to report that the fund had already accumulated £650. The current 'War Chest' (inaugurated in 2016), though not created to clear debt, is very much in the same tradition as 'The Shilling Fund' in so far as it invites fans of Batley RLFC to help boost the coffers. By May 1939 the club's debt had increased to £2,970, though the 'Shilling Fund', which stood at £792, had not been deducted from that sum. The increase in debt was primarily the consequence of a drop in gate receipts, which had fallen by £868 compared with the previous year.

Rugby Union in Batley in the 1930s

The Batley Rugby Union Club survived into the 1930s and featured players who were considered for county honours. The *Leeds Mercury*, 30th September 1930, noted that the Batley Rugby Union players, C.M Crothers, T.D. Crothers and G. Tattersfield had been selected to play in the County Trial Match. In addition to Rugby Union remaining alive in Batley it also appears that relations between the two codes was not too acrimonious. The *Leeds Mercury*, 25th September 1930, reported that on the previous evening a rugby union match between J.R. Auty's team and another local team had taken place at Mount Pleasant. It may be that such an arrangement was facilitated by the Auty family's connection with Batley C.A. and F.C. The *Batley Reporter*, 16th April 1938, also contained a report about a game at Mount Pleasant between the Batley and Wakefield Rugby Union teams, part of the proceeds of which were to be given to the Batley St. John Ambulance Brigade. Similarly, the *Yorkshire Post*, 14th April, 1930, makes reference to J. Barritt having kicked the winning goal for the Batley Rugby Union team in a match against Cleckheaton at Carlinghow Lane. Jackie Barritt was subsequently chairman of Batley C.A. and F.C., so there was cross fertilisation between codes at a local level. This transfer between the two is further highlighted by the fact that Harold Nunn, Douglas Oates and George Daniels were all signed from the same rugby union club.

One of the features that the Batley Rugby Union Club had in common with its rugby league counterpart was its financial weakness. The *Leeds Mercury*, 12th July 1934 and 3rd June 1938, reported annual losses of £49 and £50 respectively for the Batley Rugby Union Club. The former edition also drew attention to another problem, one with which Batley R.L.F.C was quite familiar, when it quoted from the annual report of the Batley Rugby Union Club:

It is time attention was given to the question of players being poached. It is serious for clubs like ours who, year after year, struggle to keep going. No club has suffered in the past more than Batley in losing players. They give the excuse that the ground is poor, but the real reason for going elsewhere is personal glory and a County Cap.

The report is obviously referring to the club's players being poached by other rugby union teams, but it may be that its author had rugby league clubs in mind too.

The Hungry Thirties

Off the Field Events

The Batley Rugby League Supporters' Club, which had been established in 1926, continued to be active in the 1930s, most interestingly, according to the *Yorkshire Post*, 8th December 1931, offering its full support for a scheme proposed by the manager of Salford which called for the introduction of summer rugby. The *Leeds Mercury*, 23rd March 1932, noted that the Batley RL Supporters' Club was promoting a Workshops Competition which included the Batley Tradesmen, Crossbank Athletic, The Fleece Hotel, Batley Shamrocks, Hilberoyd Old Boys and some teams from outside the town. John Winner, a founder member of the Supporters' Club, was instrumental in organising annual excursions to the Challenge Cup Final at Wembley and the *Leeds Mercury*, 27th February 1939, included a notice which demonstrated that Mr. Winner was organising that year's excursion in conjunction with the newspaper. Readers were informed that:

Batley football followers wishing to visit this season's Rugby League Cup Final at Wembley and travel by 'The Leeds Mercury' special Wembley excursion, should get in touch with Mr. J Winner, 102, Ealand Road, Carlinghow, Batley. Early application is advisable as the accommodation on the 'Mercury' excursion is limited.

As in previous decades, there were reports in the press that Batley RLFC would have been pleased to see go unprinted. Both the *Yorkshire Evening Post*, 14th September 1932 and *Batley News*, 17th September 1932 reported that Joe Robinson, the former Batley player, had been bound over at Batley Police Court, having pleaded guilty to stealing £5 from his sister-in-law. According to the *Batley News*, Robinson, whilst in a police cell, told Inspector Atkinson:

It is no use me sticking it out any longer. I might as well tell you I took the money. I don't know why I didn't say so at first. I don't know what made me do it. I have been in the Asylum twice and my head is funny sometimes. I am sorry I took the money.

Apparently, Robinson had been unable to find a job for twelve months and had been treated by a doctor for melancholia. Rather more prosaically, the *Leeds Mercury*, 23rd November 1932, noted that the legendary Frank Gallagher had been fined ten shillings for being drunk and disorderly in Duncan Street, Leeds. In 1935, however, members of a committee linked to the 'New Players' Fund at Batley RLFC, fell foul of the licensing laws following an event at the Albion Hotel, Batley Carr. According to the *Yorkshire Evening Post*, 15th May 1935, the five committee members were each fined £1 for consuming alcohol outside the permitted hours. The licensee, who was fined £5, said that, following a concert held for the benefit of the New Players' Fund, he had merely offered them a drink as his private guests.

Some notable and unfortunate deaths connected with the club also occurred in the 1930s. Richard Webster ('London Dick'), who had been Batley's trainer when the team won their first trophy, the Yorkshire Cup, in 1885, and who had been actively involved ever since, died in March 1931. Two well known former players died towards the end of the decade, Tom Elliker in March 1937 and Billy Wolstenholme in March 1938. The former was the legendary half-back who had played in Batley's very first game in October 1880, whilst the latter had also been a member of the original 'Gallant Youths' team which had won the Yorkshire Cup in 1885. The *Batley Reporter*, 26th March 1938, noted that Wolstenholme's funeral was attended by former teammates A. Scholes, H.

Nettleton and H. Simms. A local businessman with close connections to the club, A. J. Riley, the founder of A. J. Riley and Sons Ltd, boilermakers and engineers, died in February 1935, whilst in May of the same year Mr. J. H. Brearley, both a Batley supporter and the architect of the club's first covered stand, died at the age of seventy five.

Prior to this decade some unfortunate deaths had occurred at Mount Pleasant and sadly this theme continued into the 1930s. The *Leeds Mercury*, 19th January 1935, reported that John Armitage, aged seventy four, the caretaker of the Batley Supporters' Club, had been found dead in the pavilion at Mount Pleasant. Apparently, when Mr. Armitage had failed to return home after working at the ground his son went to look for him in the pavilion, where he found his father lying on the floor.

On a rather more positive note, the *Leeds Mercury*, 11th September 1937, noted that former Batley stalwart, George Main, had been invited by the General Purposes Committee of Batley Town Council to be the next Mayor of the borough. George, of course, had been a member of each of the Batley teams which had lifted the Challenge Cup in 1897, 1898 and 1901. He told the *Leeds Mercury* that the Challenge Cup Final game against Bradford in 1898 was the greatest match in which he ever played. The same newspaper, 29th January 1938, reported that George Main, as Mayor of Batley, had organised a reunion dinner for eleven of his former teammates who had played alongside him in those three Challenge Cup Finals, in addition to which he had arranged for the Challenge Cup to be on display at the event. Reunion events subsequently became a regular feature at Batley RLFC.

As in previous decades Mount Pleasant hosted activities other than rugby matches. Sheffield sports special *The Green Un'*, 20th August 1932, reported on the Batley C. A.

and F. C. Festival which had taken place at Mount Pleasant on that day in front of a crowd of 6,000 spectators, who had been treated to wide variety of running and cycling races involving competitors from Sheffield, Scunthorpe, Pontefract, Doncaster and other localities. The *Leeds Mercury*, 28th June 1937, noted that the thirty third Annual Show of the Batley and District Agricultural Society, which had taken place on the 26th June at Mount Pleasant, had attracted its largest attendance (5,500) for a number of years. Receipts had increased compared with the previous year, though the show entries had decreased by 132, the latter largely as a consequence of the fall in the number of mice exhibits!

The Hungry Thirties

TIMELINE: THE 1940s
UK and World Events

1940 – Food rationing is introduced in the UK
The Battle of Britain takes place between the RAF and the Luftwaffe

1941 – Hitler invades the Soviet Union
Japan attacks the US naval base at Pearl Harbour

1942 – Oxfam is founded
Montgomery's 8th Army defeats the Germans at El Alamein

1943 – Germany's troops surrender after the Battle of Stalingrad
Mussolini is deposed and Italy signs an armistice with the Allies

1944 – Operation Overlord (D Day) takes place
Paris is liberated from the Nazis

1945 – World War 2 ends
A Labour government is elected with a big majority

1946 – Churchill makes his 'iron curtain' speech in Fulton, Missouri
The BBC resumes regular TV broadcasting

1947 – The Labour government nationalises the coal industry
India and Pakistan become independent states

1948 – Israel is established as an independent state
The NHS comes into existence in the UK

1949 – NATO is established
Mao Zedong establishes The People's Republic of China

7

WORLD WAR TWO AND AFTER: THE 1940s

Context

From September 1939 until August 1945 Britain was involved in the Second World War, a war which necessitated the total mobilisation of British society in support of the war effort. Unsurprisingly, such a development had a massive impact on all areas of life in Britain, sport being no exception. The first and most obvious change was the number of men who volunteered for or were conscripted into the armed forces. Necessarily, many rugby league players were included in the vast numbers who were incorporated into the army, navy or air force. Also central to the war effort was the forging of a spirit of national unity, in pursuance of which a ground-breaking development took place. In the words of Angus Calder in his marvellous book, *The People's War* (Jonathan Cape, 1969), "It was a remarkable symptom of national unity that the amateur Rugby Union, which demanded a fifteen-a-side game, permitted its followers to play alongside men from the professional, thirteen-a-side Rugby League."

However, this spirit of co-operation did not extend beyond the war years and it was back to business as usual with regard to relations between the separate codes in the late 1940s. It had taken a cataclysmic war to dissolve the prejudices of the Rugby Union authorities, but those prejudices were reasserted once the imperatives for national unity were no longer prominent.

As occurred during the First World War, normal league competition was suspended during the Second World War and replaced with the Wartime Competition. This time, however, the matches counted as official matches, so any player who made his first appearance for a league club in a Wartime Competition game has official recognition of that appearance and is entitled to a heritage number matching that date. Though rugby league, like other team sports, was disrupted 1939-1945, the central government's view was that matches should continue to be played as part of the effort to maintain national morale by providing, where possible, distractions from the horrors and deprivations resulting from total war. Batley played twenty nine matches during the 1939-1940 season and twenty three matches during the following season in the Yorkshire League competition, and then in the Wartime League twenty two games 1941-1942, twenty one games 1942-1943 and twenty seven games during each of the final two seasons before the end of the war.

All rugby league clubs, as a result of conscription and volunteering, had to make extensive use of 'guest' players 1939-1945 in order to field a team and few, if any, made more extensive use of 'guest' players than Batley RLFC. During the war years, one hundred and twenty six 'guest' players, a few of whom returned to play for the team after the war, appeared for Batley. Charlie Eaton (Barrow), Harry Beverley (Leeds), Eric Hesketh (Wigan), Roy Francis (Barrow), Vic Hey (Leeds), Hector Gee (Leeds), Jack Walkington (Hunslet) and Billy Scott (Oldham) are just a few of the names who turned out for 'The Gallant Youths'.

Make do and Mend, 1939-1945

The use of 'guest' players is undoubtedly the most striking feature of this period. Without this facility most clubs would not have been able to field a team, so it is no surprise that there are many references in the press both to Batley's inclusion of 'guest' players and the club's frequent struggles to put together a full team.

The *Yorkshire Post* and *Leeds Mercury*, 19th March 1940, noted that Batley had been forced to postpone their match against Hull at Mount Pleasant on 22nd March because they were unable to raise a team. Conversely, the same newspaper, 25th April 1940, reported that Batley, with the assistance of four 'guest' players from Featherstone Rovers and one from Leeds, had thrashed Hull KR by thirty two points to nil. Such were the ups and downs of wartime rugby league. At the end of November 1940, a Batley team which contained no fewer than five 'guest' players from Castleford lost by twenty points to fifteen in a tight game at Mount Pleasant against Huddersfield. When Batley played Castleford on 18th October 1941, the Batley team included six 'guest' players and four players who had not been listed on the teamsheet published in the *Yorkshire Evening Post* the day before. This last minute construction of the team was by no means untypical of this period. On the same day as the game against Castleford, Batley had lent Mick Foley to Leeds for their game against Bramley at Barley Mow.

The *Yorkshire Post* and *Leeds Mercury*, 28th September 1942, reported that Batley, in their game against Leeds at Headingley, "were not certain of their team until it took the field." Apparently, Batley had been looking for a wingman five minutes before the start of the game! On some occasions Batley was only able to complete a fixture by borrowing players from their opponents on the day. The *Yorkshire Post*,

World War Two and After

25th January 1943, noted that for their game against Wigan, Batley had hoped to include four players from Widnes but unfortunately they failed to appear, the consequence of which was that Batley had to borrow players from Wigan in order to complete the fixture. In the circumstances, it is hardly surprising that Batley lost the game by sixty two points to fourteen. In January 1944, according to the *Yorkshire Post* and *Leeds Mercury*, 24th January 1944, Batley had travelled all the way to Barrow with only ten players. Fortunately, they were able to borrow three players, one of whom, Alf Marklew, had an outstanding game, from their opponents. Players, it seems, were happy to be on the field, irrespective of who they were playing for. However, not knowing from one day to the next who would be available to play for the team was not conducive to consistent performances on the field. The difficulties associated with raising a team resulted in Batley cancelling their last four fixtures of the 1942-1943 season. The *Yorkshire Evening* Post, 27th March 1943, reported a comment from Jackie Barritt, the Batley Chairman: "Often, we have not known until just before the game whether we should be able to field a full side, and the 'gates' have not been too encouraging .... In recent times, too, four of our players have gone into the services to increase the team selection difficulties we have had all the season."

Batley was not alone in curtailing its season. No less a team than Leeds decided, in March 1943, not to compete in the end of season play-offs for the top six teams. Whilst, for the most part, the use of 'guest' players worked smoothly, there was the odd glitch. The protocol was that that any club using a guest player should first acquire the permission of the parent club. The *Yorkshire Post*, 9th November 1944, observed that Bradford Northern had been fined £25 by the Emergency Committee of the Rugby League Council for fielding Bill Riches in a match against York without obtaining Batley's permission.

One direct consequence of the full mobilisation of the British workforce in support of the war effort was a fall in attendances at rugby league matches, and Batley was no exception to this trend. Key industries utilised workers round the clock and at weekends, so for many erstwhile rugby league fans attendance at a Saturday game was not an option. The *Yorkshire Post* and *Leeds Mercury*, 9th September 1940, noted that the attendance at Batley's home fixture against Leeds on the 7th September, the first Saturday of the season, had attracted a crowd of about 2,000, some considerable way short of the 'gate' for such a game. However, to put this in perspective, the average crowd for that opening day of the 1940-1941 season had only been 2,000, in addition to which the crowd at the game between Wigan and Warrington at Central Park had been less than five hundred.

In some respects Batley's performances during the war years are immaterial because of the ersatz nature of the teams fielded by the club. The number of 'guest' players that were used on a regular basis renders the idea of an authentic Batley team somewhat meaningless. Nonetheless, Batley managed to complete most of their fixtures and provide entertainment for those who were badly in need of some diversion from the demands of total war. The *Yorkshire Evening Post*, 26th September 1941, anticipated a close contest in the following day's derby game against Dewsbury at Mount Pleasant, in spite of the fact that Dewsbury hoped to field a strong team. In the event, it was in fact a closely contested game, which Batley lost by five points to four. The *Liverpool Daily Post*, 28th February 1944, reported that a Batley team which contained only two 'guest' players had put up an excellent fight against a strong Wigan team, which they restricted to a two point lead until the final minute of the game when Wigan scored a converted try, thus beating Batley by twelve points to five.

The extent to which World War 2 softened the Rugby Union's attitude to rugby league has already been noted, but what, perhaps, is more surprising is the fact that the spirit of national unity appears to have had an impact on local tribal loyalties. The *Yorkshire Evening Post*, 19th December 1942, reported the following in connection with a Batley supporter who had written to the newspaper:

He adds his hope that Dewsbury folk will find it worth their while to make the trip to Mount Pleasant on Saturdays when Dewsbury are away. " Hundreds of Rugby League men", he says, "find pleasure and entertainment at Crown Flatt when Dewsbury are at home and Batley are away. Now the Batley side is finding its feet again, there is a chance for Dewsbury followers to return the compliment."

Batley RLFC survived the war years and even made a profit of £39 during the 1943-1944 season. That its heritage was still a subject of discussion in rugby league circles in the 1940s is amply attested to by a lengthy article in the *Yorkshire Evening Post*, 20th July 1940. The newspaper, in response to a query from a member of the public, regaled its readers with a detailed account of 'Dodger' Simms heroics in single-handedly taking on nine opponents, and, for good measure provided a detailed explanation as to how Batley acquired the nickname 'The Gallant Youths'.

Performance Post-War: 1945-1950

Following the Japanese surrender on 15th August 1945, which in effect ended the Second World War, there was a swift return to normal league competition. Batley played their first game of the 1945-1946 season against Barrow on the 25th August 1945. The team's performances during the immediate post-war period 1945-1950 were somewhat uneven, though there is no doubt that Batley possessed some quality players and had, in particular, quite a formidable three-quarter line. In the first season after the war Batley registered twenty wins and four draws from thirty six league fixtures, but the following season, 1946-1947, the team achieved only fifteen victories and one draw from thirty six league games. There was a further slump to eleven wins and one draw from thirty six league fixtures during 1947-1948 season and then a dramatic improvement 1948-1949, during which season Batley recorded twenty three wins from thirty six league matches. This season, the club's most successful season of the decade, saw Batley come close to a top four finish. Unfortunately, the following season, during which the team achieved only ten victories from thirty six league games, was the club's least successful season of the decade.

Reference has been made to the fact that Batley had some outstanding individuals playing for the team during this post-war period. Eric Hesketh, Bill Riches and John Etty had all made debut appearances for Batley during the war, Hesketh as a 'guest' player in January 1943, Riches in September 1943 and Etty in March 1945. Subsequently, there were debuts for Bill Riley in February 1946, Doug Stokes, April 1946, Don Burnell, August 1947, George Palmer, January 1948, John Westbury, March 1948, Jack Perry, December 1948, Bob Kavanagh, February 1949, Gordon Harrison, September 1949 and Jonty Pilkington, November 1949. In addition Batley also had the formidable figure of Bill Hudson, who had made his debut in 1935. When Jack Perry signed for Batley in December 1948, the *Yorkshire Post* and *Leeds Mercury*, 2nd December 1948, waxed lyrical about the strength of Batley's backs: "The signing of Perry should solve one of their biggest problems. Etty has been playing on the right, but now he will be free to continue his left wing partnership with the thrustful centre Bill Riches. Perry will complete one of the best back divisions in Yorkshire, with four county men in scrum-half Burnell and threequarters Perry, Riches and Etty."

Batley's start to the first post-war season, 1945-1946, was not particularly propitious as they lost their first three matches against Barrow, Huddersfield and Keighley, conceding sixty points whilst scoring only twenty. However, as indicated above, the team recovered from this poor start and went on to win more than half of their league fixtures, losing only one third of their matches. Batley's victory against Leeds by eleven points to two at Headingley on 29th September 1945 was described in glowing terms in the *Batley Reporter*, 5th October 1945:

Exhilarating is an apt word to apply to the football seen at Headingley on Saturday, where Batley secured their third successive victory and their second away from home. The game was brimful of sparkling incidents in which both sides played fast open football, and regardless of mistakes never relaxed in their efforts to be attractive and provide thrills.... The Batley backs in particular gave a remarkably fine exhibition, the degree of efficiency attained in that respect enabling them to utilise their speed in a very impressive manner and to score three really spectacular tries.

Allowing for the hyperbole that is likely to be contained in a newspaper report about its local team, it is clear that the Batley team was one to be reckoned with. The *Batley Reporter*'s correspondent was not slow to say that Batley were fortunate to win, if he believed that to be the case. His coverage of Batley's game against Featherstone (a Batley win by fourteen points to twelve) in the *Batley Reporter*, 15th March 1946, was blunt in its assessment: "Batley were fortunate to win for had Wright converted the last try of the visitors from a position which was not very difficult, the Rovers would have shared the points and, in my opinion, deservedly so .... they [Featherstone] were the most impressive side in the first half-hour and the home lead of 9-4 at the interval was all against the run of play."

In the light of this balance, his comments in the *Batley Reporter*, 27th April 1946, about another Batley victory against Leeds, may be considered to be a reasonable assessment of the team's performance: "Batley played grand football against Leeds at Mount Pleasant on Saturday, especially in the first half when three tries were registered as the result of fast moving play characterised by crisp and sure handling."

Unfortunately, this level of performance did not continue into the next season and it was not long before there were complaints from the supporters about both the performance of the team and the policy of the directors. The *Yorkshire Post* and *Leeds Mercury*, 25th September 1946, reported that a meeting of supporters of Batley RLFC had, on the previous evening, expressed dissatisfaction with the performance of the team and called for the appointment of a full-time secretary manager. Furthermore, the newspaper recorded that at the meeting Mr George Smith had claimed that the failure to run a 'second' team was a grave error which militated against the nurturing of talented young players who could be fed through to the first team.

In spite of Batley's mediocre record in the first half of the 1946-1947 season, winning nine of their seventeen league fixtures, a crowd of 27,000 attended their game against Leeds at Headingley on 27th December 1946. Sadly, Batley lost by twenty nine points to three, though the *Yorkshire Post* and *Leeds Mercury* 28th December 1946, indicated that, as good as the Leeds team were, the score slightly flattered the home side. Nonetheless, it seems that Batley had been outplayed in most departments by a team that few opponents would be able to defeat. The following season, 1947-1948, was even more disappointing as the team won less than one third of its league fixtures. However, whilst the club may have been struggling on the field, its chairman, Jackie Barritt, was able to play an active and influential role on the Yorkshire County Rugby League Committee. The *Yorkshire Evening Post*, 15th October 1947, reported that Jackie Barritt was putting forward to the County Committee a resolution calling for the Yorkshire Cup Final to be made into an attractive spectacle. According to the newspaper Jackie Barritt said: "We should have a band – a good band- to set things going, and I want to see the players introduced to the crowd as in the New Zealand test match at Headingley. In the past it's just been a game – we want more this time, and in the future. We also want the ground which will take the biggest crowd."

Also in October 1947, Batley sold Bill Hudson to Wigan for a record fee of £2,000, having rejected Wigan's earlier offers of £900, £1,000 and £1,500. This was very good business for Batley as Hudson, who was 30 years old, had already been at the club for more than ten years. Though he was in the latter part of his career, the transfer to Wigan offered him a bigger stage on which to display his considerable talents. Nonetheless, his absence from the team was probably a major contributor to Batley's worst season since the end of the war. The following season Batley, even without Bill Hudson leading the pack, rediscovered their form and, having won sixty four percent of their league matches, just failed to reach the end of season play-offs. This was the season in which

Batley's formidable backs realised their potential and George Palmer demonstrated that he could be a worthy successor to Bill Hudson. Throughout this season Batley chalked up some impressive victories, all of which were suitably celebrated in the local press. The *Batley Reporter,* 27th August 1948, had this to say about Batley's away win at the Boulevard:

Hull people will not soon forget Batley's superb team work; brilliant forward play alike in scrimmage and in the open; ingenious half-back play from Burnell and Hesketh, who repeatedly smashed through the defence to pave the way for exhilarating and spectacular centre play, in which Riches, a dominant personality and a Hull man, played such an effective role.

The reader may raise an eyebrow at the suggestion that Hesketh and Burnell, not known for their physicality, 'smashed' their way through the opposition, but the thrust of the report is clear: Batley's performance was outstanding. The *Yorkshire Post* and *Leeds Mercury,* 23rd September 1948, reporting on Batley's victory against Huddersfield at Mount Pleasant, noted that: "Batley played spectacular football and had a great advantage at centre, where Riches was almost continuously aggressive. Hesketh was another prominent back."

Similarly, the *Batley Reporter,* 28th January 1949, was fulsome in its praise of the Batley back line in the team's victory against Wakefield by fifteen points to twelve: "A crowd of 15,000 who paid £850 was thrilled by the speed and brilliant combination of the halves and threequarters. Often movements in which Hesketh, Riches, Stokes, Etty and Perry were concerned brought the crowd to its feet, and ringing cheers greeted the dazzling and rapid exchanges as the players moved towards the visitors' line."

World War Two and After

By the end of March 1949 a top four finish was a realistic proposition for Batley and the club's determination to maintain momentum is illustrated by the decision to arrange a friendly against St Helens on 26th March. This decision was taken in order to prevent the team having no competitive action between 12th March and the 2nd April as a result of postponements due to bad weather. The decision paid off, because Batley defeated Hull KR by twenty three points to ten on the 2nd of April, thereby bringing the team within touching distance of a place in the top four.

Unfortunately, in spite of winning four of their last six games, they did not make it to the play-offs. Nevertheless, it had been a very successful season for the club, which made the following season, 1949-1950, in which Batley won only ten games, all the more painful. After the defeat by Keighley at Mount Pleasant in September 1949, the team's fourth successive loss, the *Yorkshire Post and Leeds Intelligencer*, 7th September 1949, reported that a crowd of about two hundred fans gathered outside the directors' office at Mount Pleasant demanding that the chairman, Jackie Barritt , should come out and speak to them. Apparently the police were called upon to guard the directors' office and protect those entering or leaving during the two hour period before the crowd dispersed.

Following the Keighley game, there was something of a false dawn for the fans as Batley completed a two leg victory over Halifax in the first round of the Yorkshire Cup, winning both the home and away ties. Reporting on Batley's victory by seven points to two in the second leg at Thrum Hall, the *Yorkshire Post* and *Leeds Mercury*, 14th September 1949, suggested, somewhat optimistically, that: "Batley must have completely rehabilitated themselves in the eyes of their critical supporters at Halifax last night."

According to the report: "It was, indeed, a great performance against a Halifax team which, unbeaten in the league, had every cause for confidence. The foundation was well and truly laid in the forwards for the Batley six put up a solid wall of resistance when Halifax, two points behind through Perry's goal in the tenth minute, applied furious pressure for long periods."

This victory did not provide a springboard for further success as Batley won only five of their next seventeen fixtures. The general gloom was reinforced in January 1950 when Eric Hesketh was transferred to St Helens, largely because the strain of travelling across the Pennines was becoming too arduous for him. The only compensation was that the transfer fee of £2,500 was the highest fee that Batley had ever received.

Reunions and Community events

In November 1943, Wilf Auty, a member of the Challenge Cup winning team in 1901, became Mayor of Batley, following in the footsteps of his father, Joe Auty, and another former Batley 'great' from the same era, George Main. In September of the following year Mr. Auty organised a special dinner in the Mayor's Parlour at Batley Town Hall to celebrate the seventieth birthday of 'Wattie' Davies. The latter was presented with a cheque by Wilf Auty in recognition of the voluntary public service that 'Wattie' had carried out on behalf of the town. It is clear that Batley's Mayor did not forget his teammates and the 'glory years' of Batley C.A.and F.C. because in November 1945 he hosted a reunion, again in the Mayor's Parlour, for the nine surviving members of the all-conquering cup winning teams which had won the Challenge Cup in 1897,1898 and 1901. The *Yorkshire Post*, 3rd November 1945, contained a lengthy article about the event, under the heading "The Gallant Youths Meet again at Batley". According to the report: "To encourage them the Rugby League Cup was placed in the centre of the dinner table, decorated with the old cerise and fawn colours, and to inspire them Wattie Davies, one of the nine, waved once again a cerise and fawn jersey, brought from the football treasures at his home."

The reunion, which gave the nine surviving players (F.W.H. Auty, Wattie Davies, Dai Fitzgerald, Jim Gath, Jack Goodall, George Main, Joe Oakland, Jim Phillips and Bob Spurr) the opportunity to reminisce about past glories, was a great success. Reference was made to the team's incredible defence which had only conceded 147 points in 60 Yorkshire Senior Competition games. Reunions for former players subsequently became a regular feature of the social life of Batley RLFC.

The tradition of hosting community events at Mount Pleasant was continued even during the years of World War 2. The Batley 'Holidays-at-Home' Sports Festival was held there on 29th August 1944, doubtless as part of the drive to provide some diversion from the misery and deprivation created by the war. In February 1945, history was made at Mount Pleasant when an Australian Air Force Rugby Union team played against a French Air Force Rugby Union team in aid of the 'Service Charities', after which the Mayor of Batley, Wilf Auty, hosted a dinner for the players at the Town Hall.

The Departed

The 1940s, as did previous decades, witnessed the deaths of a number of individuals associated with Batley RLFC. The *Midland Daily Telegraph*, 8th February 1940, reported the death, aged forty, of James Maurice Wale, who had played for Batley in the late 1920s having been recruited from the

Coventry Rugby Union Club. Joseph Brearley, a former Secretary of Batley C.A. and F.C., died in July 1940, aged seventy five. The *Yorkshire Evening Post*, 13th December 1944, under the heading "Batley Rugby Player Who Made History", reported the death, at the age of eighty eight, of Herbert Simms whom it described as "one of the most brilliant dodgers the game has known."

Much more tragically, Terence Douglas Stokes, the eight year old son of the Batley player Doug Stokes, died in June 1947 as the result of being hit on the head by a cricket ball.

Finally, the *Yorkshire Evening Post*, 10th March 1948, reported the death of Jack Goodall, aged seventy four. Jack had captained the teams which had won the Challenge Cup in 1897 and 1898, as well as playing in the team which won the Cup again in 1901.

World War Two and After

TIMELINE: THE 1950s
UK and World Events

1950 – The Labour Party wins a second term
in government
The Korean War begins
1951 – The Peak District is established as the first
National Park
The term 'rock n' roll' is coined by Alan Freed
1952 – Elizabeth II becomes Queen
The USA detonates the first hydrogen bomb
1953 – Watson and Crick announce their discovery of the
DNA double helix
John Christie (*10 Rillington Place*) is hanged
1954 – Roger Bannister runs the mile in under four
minutes
Great Britain wins the first Rugby League World
Cup
1955 – The Warsaw Pact is set up by the Soviet Union
Hugh Gaitskell becomes leader of the Labour party
1956 – 'Heartbreak Hotel' is a hit for Elvis Presley
The Suez Crisis takes place
1957 – The EEC is established by the Treaty of Rome
The USSR launches Sputnik 1 – an artificial
satellite
1958 – The Munich Air Crash involving the Manchester
United team
The first parking meters are installed in the UK
1959 – Fidel Castro comes to power in Cuba
The Obscene Publications Act becomes law in the
UK

8

FROM CUP FINALISTS
TO BOTTOM OF THE LEAGUE: THE 1950s

Context

In the 1950s, as Britain slowly began to recover from the damaging effects of World War 2 and rationing was finally ended, British society gradually became more affluent and a wider variety of consumer goods more readily available at affordable prices.

The 1950s was also the beginning of the TV age as increasing numbers of citizens had access to a television in their home, numbers which were boosted both by the introduction of commercial television in 1955 and the opening of ITA's Emley Moor transmitter in 1956. Ultimately, the expansion of TV transmissions had important implications for attendances at rugby league matches but for the moment the impact was limited as transmission hours were strictly regulated in the 1950s. This was also the decade in which the Queen paid an official visit to Batley. The *Birmingham Post*, 26th April 1954, noted that as part of a two day visit to Yorkshire, the Queen and the Duke of Edinburgh were going to visit Batley, Dewsbury and Morley on October 28th 1954. The visit duly took place and was, by all accounts, a roaring success.

From Cup Finalists to Bottom of the League

Unfortunately, for Batley RLFC the 1950s were not a roaring success. The first three seasons of the decade were moderately successful, Batley losing in the Yorkshire Cup Final in November 1952, but the period from September 1953 until April 1959 was one during which the club struggled to win ten games per season, finishing bottom of the league for the first time in the club's history at the end of the 1955-1956 season. It was not until the final season of the decade that there were signs of recovery. There is no doubt that Batley RLFC was damaged by the departure of Hesketh and Stokes at the beginning of the decade along with Riches and Etty in the mid-1950s. However, in spite of its distinct lack of success the team did contain some outstanding individuals such as Jack Perry, Gordon Harrison and the redoubtable George Palmer who was selected to play for England. Moreover, during the 1950s a long list of players who went on to provide very valuable service to the club made their debuts for Batley: Frank Mawson, August 1950 (110 appearances); Malcolm(Joe) Fryer, September 1951(218); Phil Walshaw, October 1951 (186 apps, 283 goals); Bill Riley, November 1951 (113); Peter Bateson, December 1952 (77 apps, 138 goals); Eric Battersby, August 1953 (126); Jack Briggs, August 1954 (239); Jim Etty, December 1954 (109 apps, 95 goals); Joe Ireland, September 1956 (186); Ian Geldard, October 1958 (228 apps, 42 tries); Jimmy Lawton, October 1958 (156 apps, 215 goals); Dave Foster, March 1959 (124); Peter McVeigh, April 1959 (79); Malcolm Shuttleworth, April 1959 (186); Brian Ward, August 1959 (189).

As indicated above, the early years of the decade were quite promising for Batley. During the first season, 1950-1951, the team registered twenty one victories and two draws from thirty six league games, reaching the semi-final of the Yorkshire Cup and third round of the Challenge Cup in which they were defeated at Wigan by sixteen points to eight. Having transferred Eric Hesketh to St Helens and Doug Stokes to Halifax, Batley were undoubtedly weakened for the first season of the new decade. However, in spite of losing by nine points to nil at Hull KR in the first leg of the first round of the Yorkshire Cup, Batley turned the tables on their opponents with a victory in the second leg at Mount Pleasant by twenty one points to four, thereby securing their passage to the second round of the competition. The *Yorkshire Evening Post*, 6th September 1950, was very positive in its assessment of Batley's performance in the second leg:

The latter part of the first half produced some of the best football Batley have played this season, with Riches, the star in the centre, scoring once after following up his own kick through and by following up another kick by Etty, who was also speedy and aggressive. The wingmen, Harrison and Perry were superior to the Rovers' pair. Harrison's speed and trickery gave him a characteristic try, and Perry proved fast and troublesome. Hull KR forwards were well matched in the open, outstanding work coming from Hattersley and Palmer for Batley.

Riches and Etty are mentioned in the above report and they were indeed crucial members of Batley's team. Both players were selected to play for the Yorkshire County team in the game against Cumberland at the end of September 1950, Riches being named as the captain. At this point in club history their importance cannot be overstated. Riches was playing brilliantly and both men had extensive experience of playing at county level, an invaluable asset for Batley. When they departed for pastures new, they left a massive hole in the team.

The semi-final of the Yorkshire Cup against Castleford at Mount Pleasant on 10th October 1950 attracted a crowd of

12,700, at that point Batley's largest post-war 'gate'. The match was drawn and Batley faced the prospect of having to face Castleford in the replay without the services of Riches, who had been chosen as a travelling reserve for the England team. In the event, Batley secured his release from the England squad, but to no avail as Batley lost the replay by thirteen points to nine. The difficulty created by the departure of Stokes was highlighted in December 1950 when John Etty expressed his dissatisfaction with his continued selection in the centre.

According to the *Yorkshire Post* and *Leeds Mercury*, 1st December 1950, he had only agreed to play in the centre as a temporary measure, pending a permanent replacement for Stokes, but since the commencement of the season he had played twenty consecutive games in the centre. The matter was partly resolved, in so far as for the remainder of the season Etty made twelve appearances on the wing and eleven in the centre, thereby playing in every single one of Batley's forty four league and cup matches. By the end of this season Jack Perry, the 'mighty atom', had kicked one hundred and twelve goals, a new club record. In recognition of this feat, and of being the first Batley player to kick one hundred goals in a season, Jack was presented with a silver salver by the board of directors and a case of dessert spoons and forks by the Supporters'Club.

In the following season, 1951-1952, Batley achieved eighteen wins and one draw from thirty six league fixtures, whilst once again they lost in the third round of the Yorkshire Cup, on this occasion by twenty seven points to eight at Hunslet. Though the team did not register as many victories as it had during the previous season, the record was no less impressive given the injuries which restricted the number of appearances by Clarrie Briggs, John Etty, Jack Perry and Gus

Steele, the last playing only in the first two games of the season. The *Yorkshire Evening Post*, 4th September 1950, noted that in their match against Leeds at Headingley Batley had "arrived riddled with injuries, with several men out of position." In spite of Batley losing by seventeen points to ten, the same report concluded that Batley's winger, Gordon Harrison, had scored the best try of the match:

An interception, made by leaping in a ruck, let him away. He beat two men with a balanced change of direction, and then roused the over 12,000 crowd to lasting applause with a glorious run, in which, carrying the ball and facing the wind, he drew away from Ryan to hurtle over the Leeds line for a superbly sprinted score.

In October 1951 Batley played the New Zealand touring team at Mount Pleasant and, though they lost the match by twenty points to thirteen, this was a game they might well have won but for the fact that their winger, Calvert, had to retire through injury twenty minutes before the end of the match. Batley had led by thirteen points to two at half-time, through tries by Calvert, Mawson and Richards and two goals by Laycock. By all accounts, had Calvert not had to leave the field, Batley would have been able to resist the tourists' fightback in the second half. In spite of a season somewhat marred by injuries, Batley finished their home fixtures on a high note with a win against the 'old enemy', Dewsbury, by seventeen points to fourteen.

Although Batley reached the Yorkshire Cup final in November 1952, the 1952-1953 season was not a particularly successful one with regard to performances in league matches as the team registered only fourteen wins and two draws from thirty six league games. In retrospect, this season can be seen to mark the beginning of a major slump which ultimately led to Batley finishing bottom of the league for the first time in the club's history. A season which had begun promisingly with seven wins from twelve league and cup fixtures ended somewhat ignominiously with only three wins from the last eleven league games. Nonetheless, prior to the start of the 1952-1953 season there was some very good news for Bill Riches. The *Batley Reporter*, 2nd August 1952, noted that Bill's benefit fund was on course to exceed £700, a tidy sum in the early 1950s. Apparently, having received a cheque for £607 from the Batley directors he was later presented with a cheque for £106/12s from the Batley Rugby League Supporters' Club, with another cheque for £40 on its way from the West Ardsley branch of the Supporters' Club. It is clear from the comments that were made at the presentation organised by the Supporters' Club that its members were extremely grateful for the service that Bill Riches had already performed for Batley RLFC.

Batley progressed to the Yorkshire Cup Final against Huddersfield on 15th November 1952 via victories against Dewsbury, Keighley and Featherstone. Though the *Batley Reporter*, 15th November 1952, was optimistic about Batley's chances in the final, the general consensus was summed up in the *Yorkshire Post* and *Leeds Mercury*, 15th November 1952: "Huddersfield have been strong favourites to win the trophy for the eleventh time ever since they beat Halifax in the semi-final. Their victory at Batley in a league match last Saturday confirmed the impression that their superior combined speed and individual brilliance will take them to victory."

Even the *Batley Reporter* acknowledged Huddersfield were the faster team and that Batley could not afford to waste any scoring chances. In the event, Batley lost the match by eighteen points to eight, but it was not so much the action on the pitch which excited discussion as the conditions under which the game was played. J. W. Harrison, writing in the *Batley Reporter*, 22nd November 1952, claimed:

It was, shall I say, football in silhouette. I have never before seen football played under such conditions before. A murky, misty dark atmosphere came over the field at four o' clock – threequarter time – and almost completely obliterated the play from the spectators.

The Batley players I could not see, and my following of the play depended upon the movements of the white jerseyed Huddersfield men and then only when they came near the touchline on the official side.

Batley were without Perry, absent through injury, and suffered an additional blow when Westbury was forced to retire in the second half because of an ankle injury. Batley fought hard and right up to the end of the match with the result being in doubt up to the last few minutes when Valentine sealed Huddersfield's triumph with a try that was converted by Devery. The only other highlight of the 1952-1953 season was Batley's historic victory by twelve points to nine against Wigan at Central Park on 20th December 1952. The victory was historic because it was Batley's first ever win at Central Park. The *Yorkshire Evening Post*, 27th December 1952, in pointing out that Batley had played a rugby league match at Wigan for the first time in January 1896, noted that:

They failed to get a try in that 1896 game – last Saturday, when for almost half the game they were a man short, they got two tries, and little Perry, who scored one of them, popped the ball over the bar three times to complete the score of twelve points, and to give Batley as much encouragement as they can have drawn from one game in the last quarter of a century, at all events.

From Cup Finalists to Bottom of the League

Unfortunately, this historic victory did not provide Batley with the impetus for further success as the team lost eight of their next twelve matches. One of those losses was at home to Leeds at the end of January 1953, but this match is best recalled not so much for the result as for the injury suffered by the Leeds 'golden boy', Lewis Jones. This stylish centre, who had been recruited by Leeds from Welsh Rugby Union in November 1952 for a record signing on fee of £6,000, had suffered a succession of injuries since he made his debut in the professional game. In the match against Batley, following a tackle by John Etty, Jones fell awkwardly and suffered a double fracture of his left forearm.

The Lean Years and Rock Bottom 1953-60

The decline in the team's performance which had been visible 1952-1953 continued into the following season in which Batley secured only thirteen victories from thirty six league matches, in addition to which they failed to progress beyond the first round of either cup competition. Undoubtedly, the team sorely missed the powerful play of Bill Riches, who had departed to play for Hull, his home city. However, there were still some stirring performances by individual players and occasional unexpected victories. Moreover, in January 1954 Batley signed a seventeen year old who was subsequently, after an intervening spell at Featherstone, to become a future star. That teenager was Norman Field, a future international winger equipped with one of the most devastating hand-offs the game has witnessed.

In January 1954 Batley secured a surprise win against Hunslet at Parkside. Peter Bateson's kicking was the decisive factor, but the *Yorkshire Post* and *Leeds Mercury*, 11th January 1954, reserved special praise for Gordon Harrison's speed and opportunism in scoring two tries. Batley then, to everyone's surprise, beat Leeds by twenty points to thirteen in the first leg of the first round of the Challenge Cup at Headingley in February 1954 before losing on aggregate after the home fixture, a match which attracted a crowd of 15,000. In its report of the first leg fixture, the *Yorkshire Evening Post*, 8th February 1954, had special plaudits for the Batley forwards, and George Palmer in particular.

Prior to these two fixtures, Tom Shirtliffe had been transferred from Batley to Leeds. Unfortunately, Shirtliffe managed to play only four matches for Leeds before he collapsed on the field, thereby ending his career. Towards the end of the 1953-1954 season Batley registered an unexpected victory against Huddersfield by eleven points to three at Mount Pleasant. It was notable both for an outstanding performance by Bill Riley and the fact that, though playing up the slope in the second half, Batley's defence held tight. The team also put up a creditable fight in their home match against Wigan in April 1954, just losing by ten points to seven. Nonetheless, the general dissatisfaction with performances during the past season was summed up by the quote from J.S. Barritt, the president of Batley C.A. and F.C., reported in the *Yorkshire Post* and *Leeds Mercury*, 15th July 1954:

In some of the games where our opponents ran up big scores had our team shown more spirit and more of the will to win, the scoring levels of our opponents would have been drastically curtailed. It looked as if some players were content to draw losing pay.

If this broadside from Jackie Barritt was intended to result in improved performances during the upcoming season, it manifestly failed to achieve its objective as Batley won only seven of their thirty six league fixtures in the 1954-1955 season. In fact the team had only two victories from the first twelve league matches and only one from the last twelve. One of those first two victories was an away win at the recently formed Blackpool Borough, courtesy of two tries by Gerry Cox, who almost missed playing in the match. According to the *Yorkshire Post* and *Leeds Mercury*, 18th August 1954: "He had stayed in Blackpool overnight and he arrived at the dressing room just as Batley officials had decided that the call of the sea had proved too strong for him and were reorganising their forces to fill the vacancy."

Readers may draw their own conclusions as to what the euphemistic expression 'the call of the sea' actually meant. At the beginning of October 1954 the 43 year old legendary player, Gus Risman, made his first appearance for Batley, having been signed on a match-to-match basis. It did not take Risman long to make his mark as he kicked seven goals in his first game, a victory against Doncaster at Mount Pleasant by twenty six points to ten on 2nd October 1954. In all, Risman only played nine games for Batley, mainly as a full back, but on two occasions he wore the number six jersey. This arrangement was never likely to last very long, but at least it gave Batley fans the opportunity to see a truly legendary figure in action, one who, in spite of his advanced years, managed to kick twenty goals in nine matches.

In spite of having won only three of their first fifteen league matches, the one positive note for Batley at this juncture of the 1954-1955 season was that they had conceded fewer points than Huddersfield, Yorkshire's leading club at the end of November 1954. In early December 1954 Batley lost to Hunslet at Parkside by fourteen points to nil and the *Yorkshire Post and Leeds Intelligencer*, 6th December 1954, pulled no punches in it assessment of Batley's performance. According to the newspaper the Batley team, completely overwhelmed by Hunslet, was bereft of any constructive ideas and, aside from George Palmer, offered no threat whatsoever. The situation went from bad to worse at the end of January 1955 when, as a consequence of Batley's financial difficulties, John Etty, the team's star winger, was sold to Oldham for a fee of £2,650. This enforced sale was a major blow for the Batley fans for whom John had become something of an iconic figure during the period since he made his debut in March 1945. John's transfer occurred less than two months before he would have been entitled to a benefit, one that was richly deserved. However, in recognition of his service to Batley RLFC, the directors presented John with a cheque for £650 in lieu of his benefit. Towards the end of the 1954-1955 season the *Yorkshire Post* and *Leeds Mercury*, 13th April 1955, struck a more positive note in its report about Batley's defeat at Keighley by twenty three points to eighteen. According to the report:

Batley if anything, impressed more as a team. They played a more purposeful cohesive game, and never gave up, despite being 15-3 down at one stage .... Stand-off Cox, centre Riley and prop forward Palmer were the main springs in the lively Batley side.

Sadly, these green shoots did not flower because the following season 1955-1956, was the one in which Batley, for the first time in its history, finished bottom of the league, with just seven wins and one draw from thirty four league fixtures.

It was a dismal season in which Batley conceded at least twenty points on no fewer than seventeen occasions, and this was when a try was still only worth three points. How the once mighty had fallen. One of the few highlights of this season was a home win against Wakefield Trinity by fifteen points to five at the end of October 1955, courtesy of three tries by 'Nobby' Clark. The same player also ensured that

From Cup Finalists to Bottom of the League

Batley fans could enjoy their Boxing Day dinner after he scored two more in the away victory against Dewsbury on 26th December. On a slightly more bizarre note, the *Lancashire Evening Post*, 7th December 1955, reported the following:

It was revealed today that a dramatic strike threat by Bramley rugby league players, ten minutes before the kick-off in the Mount Pleasant game with Batley was averted only through a frank dressing room discussion between officials and players.

The kick-off was due at 2:30pm. At 2:20pm the players informed the officials that they wanted a new bonus scale which would provide each man with ten shillings on a progressive system. They were told that if they refused to play taxis would be sent to collect the second team.

The following three seasons, 1956-1957, 1957-1958 and 1958-1959, rendered only twenty eight victories from one hundred and fourteen league fixtures. In the first of those, Batley incurred twelve straight losses before they won a match, and during the 1957-1958 season they lost their last nine fixtures. The 1958-1959 season was slightly better in that Batley managed to reach the semi-final of the Yorkshire Cup in which they lost to Wakefield Trinity by twenty one points to thirteen. Nonetheless, this cup run was undoubtedly the high point of this season as Batley won only one of their last fifteen league fixtures.

Perhaps most disappointing of all was the fact that during each of those three seasons there were at least five occasions when Batley conceded thirty points or more. Indeed, during the 1957-1958 season the team allowed the opposition to score more than sixty points on two occasions. The first was a loss by sixty eight points to nineteen against Huddersfield in a Yorkshire Cup match in August 1957 and the second by sixty one points to twelve against Wakefield in April 1958.

During this lean period there were occasions when the gloom was temporarily lifted, such as when in November-December 1956 Batley achieved three successive wins against Huddersfield, Liverpool City and Widnes. The Liverpool City fans were not happy with some of the referee's decisions and, according to the *Liverpool Echo*, 3rd December 1950, gathered outside the changing rooms at the end of the match to make their displeasure known. The upshot was that, in order to ensure his safety, the referee was escorted from the ground via some allotments. These victories were small crumbs of comfort for the long-suffering Batley fans. That is not to say that no effort was made to strengthen the team, but as usual Batley was operating within tight financial constraints. New players, some of them local lads like Eddie Redfearn and Malcolm Shuttleworth, were drafted into the squad, whilst others like Ian Geldard and Jimmy Lawton were acquired from other teams. Eric Batten, as the coach for a brief period, tried to improve fitness levels within the team, whilst Frank Watson and Arthur Staniland, working in partnership as coaches, strove to get the best from the players.

One of Batley's new recruits in 1956, Joe Ireland, distinguished himself in another sport. In 1957 Joe won the Bisley Master Shot badge by scoring 298 points out of 300 and the Bisley Expert Shot badge with 295 points out of 300. In 1958 George Palmer was awarded a 'benefit' for ten years service at Batley RLFC. George, who was from Hull, played the whole of his career for Batley, the team to which he remained loyal for the rest of his life.

The final season of the decade, 1959-1960, was a rather more successful one for Batley. The team registered eighteen wins and three draws from thirty eight league fixtures, thus lifting the spirits of their loyal fans. Moreover, though this was a decade in which successive Batley teams struggled to make an impact, it was also one in which the record for the number of goals kicked in a season was broken on three occasions; initially by Jack Perry in 1951, then by Phil Walshaw in 1958 and finally by Stan Thompson in 1959.

Sadly, this was also the decade in which three famous Batley players died: Joe Oakland and Tom Elliker in 1951 and George Ramsbottom in 1952. All three had made major contributions to the evolution of Batley C.A. and FC.

The Club's Profile and Financial Affairs

Though, for the most part, Batley teams failed to distinguish themselves on the field of play during the 1950s, some of the club's officials were active in connection with other aspects of the sport. Jackie Barritt, who in July 1950 was re-elected for the twelfth time as chairman of Batley RLFC, was both an international selector and a member of a number of important committees. In January 1954 Mr Barritt, as vice-chairman of the Rugby League Management Committee, was part of deputation to Customs and Excise calling for the exemption of Rugby League from the Entertainments Tax on the same basis as the exemption given to cricket. According to the *Yorkshire Post*, 19th December 1951, Ewart Earnshaw, a director at Batley RLFC, had urged the Yorkshire Rugby League Council to allow the televising of rugby league matches. Just over two years later, the *Western Mail and South Wales News*, 8th January 1954, reported that the Rugby League Council had, on the previous day, agreed to the televising of as many rugby league matches as possible.

In December 1952, however, Batley RLFC was in the news for the wrong reasons. Both the *Batley Reporter*, 13th December 1952 and the *Yorkshire Post* and *Leeds Mercury*, 9th

December 1952, reported that four directors of Batley C.A and F.C. had been removed from the board of directors at an extraordinary meeting of shareholders. The reason for their removal was, apparently, the irregular use of proxy votes in the election of new directors in July 1952. On a more positive note with regard to the profile of Batley C.A. and F.C., the *Yorkshire Post*, 4th February 1954, announced that The Central Yorkshire Cricket League Committee had agreed to play a West Indies X1 at Mount Pleasant in the summer.

In the early 1950s Batley was still, on occasions able to attract crowds in excess of 10,000, most notably 12,700 in October 1950 for the game against Castleford and 13,500 in November 1951 for the game against Bradford Northern. However, by October 1955 the club's finances were in such a parlous state that the *Yorkshire Post* and *Leeds Mercury*, 12th October 1955, included an article under the headline 'Batley Future Uncertain.' According to this newspaper the Batley directors had issued a statement which said:

Unless our team attract more support we shall be faced with the problem of either raising money by some other means or going out of existence. Unless success in some way comes quickly the end might not be far off.

The hyperbolic tone may have been designed to spur the public into action, but it is clear that the club faced serious financial difficulties. A variety of activities, including a grand Ball at the Town Hall sponsored by the Raymar Carpet Company, were organised for the purpose of raising additional funds, but the fundamental problem remained; the club needed to get more spectators coming through the turnstiles. At the end of the 1957-1958 season Batley had incurred a financial loss of more than £1,000.

From Cup Finalists to Bottom of the League

The situation improved somewhat during the following season, in which there was a thirty three percent increase in 'gates' and a loss of less than £300 over the season. A further indication that there was a gradual improvement in the club's financial position came in December 1959, when the Finance Committee of the Rugby League approved Batley's application for a £1,200 loan to improve their covered accommodation. According to the *Coventry Evening Telegraph*, 2nd December 1959, York had been refused a loan until the club provided further information about its financial situation.

The Club and the Community

The Batley and District Agricultural Society continued to hold its Annual Show at Mount Pleasant during the 1950s in spite of the gradual decline of agricultural activity in the locality. Adverts in the local press announced that in addition to dogs, horses, rabbits, cattle, agricultural produce, a variety of birds and handicrafts being on show, there would also be mounted sports taking place.

In September 1952, Batley RLFC began broadcasting live commentaries of matches at Mount Pleasant to patients in Staincliffe General Hospital. The first broadcast was the Yorkshire Cup match against Keighley on Tuesday 23rd September 1952. The *Batley Reporter*, 27th September 1952, noted that one potential snag had arisen in connection with the broadcasts – the commentaries on Saturday afternoon would coincide with the hospital's visiting hours. One patient offered the obvious solution that the visiting hours would have to be changed!

TIMELINE: THE 1960s
UK and World Events

1960 – OPEC is established
John F Kennedy wins the American Presidential election
1961 – Yuri Gagarin becomes the first human to travel into outer space
Birth control pills become available on the NHS
1962 – The first episode of *Z Cars* is broadcast on the BBC
The Cuban Missile Crisis takes place
1963 – John F Kennedy is assassinated
The first episode of *Dr Who* is broadcast on the BBC
1964 – *Top of the Pops* is broadcast for the first time
Harold Wilson becomes Prime Minister
1965 – Ian Brady and Myra Hindley are arrested and charged with murder
The Race Relations Act makes public racial discrimination illegal
1966 – Indira Gandhi becomes Prime Minister of India
England win the FIFA World Cup
1967 – Jeremy Thorpe becomes leader of the Liberal Party
The first heart transplant operation is completed
1968 – Martin Luther King is assassinated
The Abortion Act comes into effect in the UK (except Northern Ireland)
1969 – The Kray twins are convicted of murder
Neil Armstrong and Buzz Aldrin set foot on the moon

9

IN THE DOLDRUMS – THE 1960s

The improvement in the team's performance in the final season of the 1950s may have led some fans to believe that a revival was on the horizon. If so, those fans were to be sadly disappointed as the following decade was essentially a repeat of the previous one with regard to performance and results.

That is not to say that during the 1960s there were no outstanding performances by individual players or surprise victories against much stronger opponents, but rather that, for the most part, there was little for the fans to cheer about. Over the whole of the decade, Batley only managed to win ninety nine games from the three hundred and forty six league games that they played. As in the 1950s the middle of decade was particularly punishing. From the beginning of the 1965-1966 season to the end of the 1967-1968 season Batley registered only sixteen victories from one hundred and two league matches, an unenviable record.

The 'Gallant Youths' made quite a promising start to the first season of the new decade, winning nine of their first fourteen league matches and six of their last ten. However, the season was marred by nine consecutive defeats incurred between the end of November 1960 and the middle of January 1961. Batley's most notable victories during this season were against Hull, Huddersfield (the double) and

Wakefield Trinity. The last victory, by five points to two at Mount Pleasant in September 1960, was a major coup as Wakefield had one of the strongest teams in the league, with players such as Gerry Round, Neil Fox, Alan Skene, Ken Rollin and Derek Turner and were also the current holders of the Challenge Cup. The 'gate' for the match was 8,000, a measure of Wakefield's stature within the sport. Harry Beevers, writing in the *Batley News,* 25th September 1960, attributed Batley's victory primarily to their teamwork combined with an inspirational performance by the captain, Bob Kelly. According to Harry: "They passed the ball in exhilarating fashion, they tackled vigorously and without relaxing their effort and they provided the cover when it was needed. In contrast, the cup holders were slow, they had no supporting play, and they adopted the wrong tactics with the slope advantage."

Mr Beevers, highlighting the telling contributions made by Billy Pratt, Peter Armstead and Brian Ward, concluded that though Batley's victory was a big surprise it was no fluke. Another one of those nine wins from the first fourteen league games was a thrilling away win, by fifteen points to thirteen, secured in the final minutes of the game at Salford in October 1960. Harry Beevers, in his column in the *Batley News,* 22nd October 1960, expressed the view that Batley's margin of victory did not do justice to their overall superiority in the game. Harry reserved particular praise for the combined play of Brian Ward and Brian Pratt on Batley's right flank. Unfortunately, as indicated earlier, Batley were unable to build on their promising start to the season and their poor form in mid-season cost them dearly.

During the following season, 1961-1962, Batley registered only nine victories and two draws from thirty six league matches. More worryingly, there was a period from mid-January 1962 to mid-April 1962 during which the team failed to secure a single victory from thirteen consecutive league matches. There were also ten matches in this season in which Batley failed to score a try, an ominous sign for the immediate future. There was a slight improvement in results during the 1962-1963 season as the team chalked up fourteen wins and two draws from thirty four league games, one of the highlights being a home win against Wakefield Trinity by thirteen points to eleven. The team also finished the season relatively strongly with six victories from the last ten matches. If the fans were hoping that this augured well for the following season, then they were soon to be disappointed as Batley lost six of their opening seven matches in the 1963-1964 season. In fact there was a clear dip in performance from the previous season as Batley secured only eleven wins from thirty four league matches, registering eleven consecutive losses in their last eleven league games.

The only real highlights of this season, in which there were fifteen games in which Batley failed to score a try, were the away victories against Huddersfield and Halifax, the latter in the first round of the Challenge Cup. This victory against Halifax, current holders of the Yorkshire Cup, was certainly a major surprise, Halifax being one of the teams that were strongly fancied to win the trophy. Once again Harry Beevers, writing in the *Batley News*, 15th February 1964, covered the encounter in detail. According to Harry:

Batley won because they revealed defensive work the like of which has not been seen at Thrum Hall in a very long time....

Not only did Batley hold Halifax but they also contributed quite a good portion to an entertaining game. Forwards and backs alike threw themselves wholeheartedly into this battle of wits, but always the defences prevailed.

Malcolm Shuttleworth secured the win with an opportunistic try, but according to Mr Beevers Batley's outstanding player was Ian Geldard who constantly troubled the Halifax defence with his swerving runs. This unexpected victory certainly gave the Batley fans something to cheer about and raised expectations for their second round clash with Hunslet at Mount Pleasant at the end of February 1964. Unfortunately, in front of a crowd of 11,000, Batley were not able to overcome their opponents, losing in the end by fourteen points to six in a closely fought game. Sadly, Batley's win at Halifax at the beginning of February turned out to be their last victory of the season.

Batley's downward spiral continued into the 1964-1965 season in which they won only ten of their thirty six league fixtures. By the time Batley faced Hull KR away in the first round of the Challenge Cup at the beginning of February 1965, the 'Gallant Youths' had won only six of the twenty three matches they had played, one of their many defeats being a forty one points to thirteen thrashing by Hull KR at Craven Park. Few, if any, anticipated Batley's victory by seven points to five. Just as Halifax had been second favourites to win the Challenge Cup in 1964, Hull KR were being identified as potential winners by many pundits in 1965. In the end it was a drop goal by Peter Fox, who had recently returned from an unhappy stint at Hull KR, which made the difference between the teams.

A key to Batley's win was their ability to keep possession of the ball in a match that pre-dated the six tackle rule. It was estimated that Hull KR handled the ball no more than a dozen times during the second half. Once again it was Malcolm Shuttleworth who scored Batley's try, in addition to which their forwards, against all expectations, mastered the powerful Hull KR pack. The only other performances worth noting in this season were the four all draw against Wakefield Trinity and the defeat of Featherstone Rovers by fourteen points to two, both matches taking place at Mount Pleasant.

The period stretching from the beginning of the following season until the end of the 1967-1968 season was one of the least successful in the club's history. The statistics for the 1965-1966 season tell a dismal story, as Batley recorded only six victories and two draws from thirty four league fixtures, losing ten consecutive matches at the end of the season. Furthermore, there were sixteen games in which the team failed to score a try in addition to seventeen occasions when they conceded at least twenty points. Batley's highest score during this season was only sixteen points, achieved in a home victory against York in January 1966.

There was no improvement in the team's overall performance in the following season, during which, for the second consecutive season, Batley won only six matches from their thirty four league fixtures, failing to register their first victory until 8th October 1966, after suffering eight consecutive defeats in the league and one in the first round of the Yorkshire Cup. In addition to this very poor start to the season, Batley also won only two of their final ten league matches. There was also no yuletide cheer for the Batley fans as the team lost both the home and away games against arch-rivals, Dewsbury. The heaviest defeats during the 1966-1967 season were inflicted by Castleford, Leeds, Hull, Hull KR and Wakefield Trinity, who between them notched up one hundred and fifty nine points as against the fifty four scored by Batley in these five fixtures.

Not only was the next season, 1967-1968, no better with regard to results, it was actually worse. Batley registered four wins and one draw in thirty four league matches. The team conceded one hundred and thirty four points in the first three league games of the season, including a record defeat by seventy eight points to nine at Wakefield. Batley won only one of their first twenty league matches, a very surprising victory by thirteen points to twelve against Leeds at Mount Pleasant, the win being secured by a drop goal from Terry Gorman There was little else for the fans to cheer about as Batley conceded twenty points or more on seventeen occasions, including three occasions on which more than forty points were conceded. Apart from the very poor results, the main talking point in this season was the brawl which took place during the opening fixture against Bradford Northern in August 1967. The *Batley News*, 26th August 1967, featured the following detailed report of the incident:

In view of the widespread publicity given to the incident, the Batley version of what took place ought to be given It has been alleged that Berwyn Jones, the Bradford player, was attacked by a Batley substitute who was sitting on the trainer's bench, and others joined in, including Fearnley (Bradford coach) and Roberts (international prop forward), who was not playing in the game, and a number of Batley reserve players from the crowd.

Within seconds the incident flared up and it has been alleged that fists and boot were freely used.

From the Batley angle it is said that while Doyle was sitting on the bench Jones went over the touchline and almost into the railings. Doyle put his arm out to protect himself and "may have called Jones a name." Jones struck him, the Batley man hit back , and very soon Fearnley and Roberts were in the fray.

The report went on to say that independent witnesses, though their independent status was not explained in the article, claimed that the fracas would have fizzled out very quickly had it not been for the intervention by Fearnley and Roberts. In the event, though Batley had previously received an official warning from the Rugby League Council following crowd trouble, no serious action was taken against the club.

Mercifully, during the final two seasons of the decade results began to improve, allowing for the fact that the team was starting from a low base. During the 1968-1969 season Batley secured eight victories and one draw from thirty four league matches, a poor set of results but still an improvement on the results from the previous three seasons. More significantly, perhaps, there were only five games in which Batley failed to score a try. The high point was a home victory against Huddersfield by twelve points to six in December 1968, whilst the low point, with regard to results, was undoubtedly the sixty three points to eleven trouncing by Leeds at Headingley in April 1969.

The other low point, unconnected with results, was the death of the Dewsbury player, John Davies, following his collapse on the field during the derby game at Crown Flatt in March 1969. The final season of the decade, 1969-1970, was Batley's most successful season of the 1960s as the team notched up fifteen wins and one draw from thirty four league fixtures. Furthermore, during this season there was only one game in which Batley failed to score a try.

There is no doubt that the team was more competitive, largely as a consequence of the presence of players such as Phil Doyle, Stan Gittins, Terry Gorman, Geoff Marsh, Keith Toohey and Tommy Martyn and Phil Holmes (debut January 1970). Thus Batley were able to beat Swinton, Wakefield, Warrington and Widnes, and put up a good fight against St Helens before succumbing by eight points to seven. This was also the season in which Trevor Walker, the Batley prop, scored seventeen tries, claimed, at the time, as a world record for a prop. Trevor's technique was unfailingly simple. Using his great bulk and low centre of gravity he would crash over the line, taking with him several opponents and, occasionally, a member of his own team who happened to get in the way!

Amidst the gloom and despondency generated by the results during the 1960s it is easy to overlook the outstanding contributions made by individual players.

In the early years of the decade, Norman Field, having returned from a short spell at Featherstone, made his mark to such an extent that he was selected to play for Great Britain against Australia in October 1963. Though this was his only international appearance, there is little doubt that he would have won more caps had he been playing for a more successful team than Batley. Norman retired from the game in 1964 at the relatively young age of twenty seven. Ian Geldard, frequently the one player to shine amidst a poor performance by the team, having given great service to the club since his debut in October 1958, bowed out in 1967. During the mid and late-1960s Phil Doyle, a skilful and intelligent loose forward, bamboozled many an opponent with his exquisite dummy and, unsurprisingly was selected to play for the county team. Several pundits shared the view that had Doyle been a yard or two quicker, he would have been selected to play for Great Britain. Reference has already been made to Stan Gittins, Tommy Martyn and Terry Gorman, the last being the one who brought the other two from Lancashire to Mount Pleasant. Both Gittins and Martyn were outstanding players, the former making his debut in October 1967 and the latter in September 1969. Stan Gittins, who made 138 appearances for Batley, though slight in stature, was unerringly safe under the high ball, irrespective of the pressure to which he was subjected. Tommy Martyn was a tearaway second row forward who, though he made only sixty appearances for Batley, had a powerful impact on the team. It was clear from the outset that Batley would struggle to hold on to Martyn, particularly given the state of the club's finances, and that proved to be the case when he was sold to Leigh in 1971.

In addition to players such as Field, Doyle and Martyn, there were other individuals who made their debuts for Batley in the 1960s before going on to provide valuable service to the club: Alec Dick, February 1960 (117 appearances); Len Johnston, January 1961 (105); Dave Rayner, August 1964 (128); Trevor Barlow, August 1964 (100); Ernie Hepworth, December 1966 (188); Trevor Walker, August 1967 (111); Geoff Marsh, September 1969 (188, 60 tries); John Fox, March 1969 (286) ; Keith Toohey, October 1969 (85 , 225 goals); Alan Watts, October 1969 (333).

Finances

Given Batley's results during the 1960s and the subsequent fall in 'gate' receipts, it is hardly surprising that the club's financial position was precarious throughout the decade. Such were the tight margins within which the directors were operating that any unanticipated costs stretched the budget to its limit and beyond.

Consequently, it was rumoured that, as a result of the pilfering of coke from the coke store, the players had to dip into their own pockets to ensure that there was sufficient fuel to heat the boiler which provided hot water for the players' bath. When Batley set out to sign Jack Pycroft from Oldham in 1965, the money had to be raised from a variety of sources including the directors, The Supporters' Club and an appeal fund. It has even been suggested by a former Batley player that the members of a team against which Batley played donated their match fees to the appeal fund.

By the 1960s Batley's ground was badly in need of refurbishment and modernisation, particularly with regard to the changing facilities for the players. The dual purpose pavilion, adjacent to the cricket field, was in a very poor state of repair and some distance from the rugby pitch. The facilities were a disincentive to those who might be considering signing to play for Batley. As had been the case in the 1950s, the club utilised a variety of money raising schemes, ranging from jumble sales and waste paper collection to a charity ball at the Town Hall. What was certain was that once Batley had a marketable player they would eventually have to sell him to generate some ready cash.

Eventually, courtesy of the assistance of many volunteers who donated their labour and expertise free of charge, supporters, officials and players amongst them, the club was able to modernise the facilities. The changing rooms were relocated to a space underneath the Short Stand and the turnstiles were re-sited beyond the lower boundary of the cricket field to allow immediate access to the football ground. In addition, the Miner's Welfare Club, later to become The Taverners, was bought for use as a social club. The new facilities were 'christened' on 16th August 1969, when a crowd of more than 2,000 turned up to watch Batley play Hull KR in the second round of the Yorkshire Cup.

Now all that was needed was for the results to match the new facilities. As indicated earlier, this final season of the decade was a relatively successful one compared with what had gone before.

In the Doldrums

TIMELINE: THE 1970s
UK and World Events

1970 – 18-year-old citizens can now vote in UK elections
Edward Heath becomes Prime Minister

1971 – The Ibrox Disaster – 66 spectators are killed at
Ibrox Stadium, Glasgow
The Old Grey Whistle Test is broadcast for the first
time

1972 – The NUM begins a strike which lasts for seven
weeks
Bangladesh becomes independent from Pakistan

1973 – The introduction of VAT in the UK
The jury returns an open verdict in the 'Bloody
Sunday' inquest

1974 – Ted Heath resigns as Prime Minister
Richard Nixon, US President resigns over
Watergate Scandal

1975 – Margaret Thatcher becomes leader of the
Conservative Party
The Vietnam War ends

1976 – The first commercial Concorde flight takes off
Jimmy Carter wins the US Presidential election

1977 – Fleetwood Mac release their album *Rumours*
Silver Jubilee celebrations are held in the UK

1978 – The 'Yorkshire Ripper' murders Helen Rytka, his
eighth victim
John Paul II becomes Pope

1979 – A nuclear accident occurs at Three Mile Island,
Pennsylvania
Margaret Thatcher becomes the UK's first female
Prime Minister

10

DISAPPOINTMENT AFTER EARLY PROMISE – THE 1970s

The story of Batley RLFC in the 1970s is, in the wake of the 1950s and 1960s, an all too familiar one as the team, following a promising start to the new decade, subsequently struggled to win more than a handful of games per-season. The percentage of wins from the total number of league matches played in the 1970s was marginally higher than it had been in the 1960s, but this was minor consolation as Batley still won less than one third of the league fixtures they played during the decade. This was also the decade in which a major quarrel occurred between the Supporters' Club and the board of directors, a quarrel which was reported in the national press.

The improvement in the team's performance which had taken place in the 1969-1970 season continued into the ensuing season, 1970-1971. Inspired by the efforts of Doyle, Gittins, Martyn, Marsh (19 tries), Holmes and Toohey (75 goals), Batley obtained seventeen victories and two draws from thirty four league games. Amongst the matches that Batley failed to win there were five that were lost by a narrow margin. Most encouragingly, in ten of the games played Batley scored at least four tries, whilst their longest losing sequence only stretched to four matches. Batley's results enabled them to participate in the top sixteen play-offs at the end of the season, though their involvement was brief as they were beaten by twenty eight points to nil against Leeds at Headingley. 1970-1971 was also the season in which 'Ziggy' Piwinski, Dave Brooke, Steve Grinhaff and Dave Secker were signed and integrated into the team. Steve Grinhaff may very well qualify as the Batley player whose name was most frequently misspelt in the match programmes at 'away' fixtures. Steve has said that on one occasion he was listed in the match programme as 'Grin Offenstein'. Unfortunately, he couldn't recall at which club this listing had taken place.

The most anticipated match of the season was the Challenge Cup tie against Wigan at Mount Pleasant in January 1971, a match which was televised. Harry Beevers, previewing the match in the *Batley News*, 21st January 1971, wrote: "It's a game that has caught the imagination of the fans throughout the R.L. world, and with the aid of B.B.C. Television will be watched by many thousands."

Harry believed that if Batley maintained their recent form they might be able to beat Wigan. He reported that the players, should they win, would collect a substantial bonus payment. During the week prior to the fixture, every effort was made to ensure that the pitch was in good condition. It was rolled for about six hours before straw was laid on top of the surface in order to protect it from the frost. In the event, Batley did not manage to achieve a famous cup victory as they lost the match by thirteen points to four. Nonetheless, Batley did not disgrace themselves, restricting Wigan to one try and matching their opponents in the battle of the forwards. Wigan scored their try in the opening minutes of the game but according to Harry Beevers' report in the *Batley News*, 28th January 1971: "What must have been a source of general satisfaction to Batley officials and supporters was the manner in which they so completely 'bottled up' the league leaders after that early shock. Only on one other occasion did a Wigan attack reach the Batley line, and defenders were sufficiently alert to get the man with the ball over the 'dead' ball line."

The following season, 1971-1972, was a disaster with regard to results as Batley registered only five wins and two draws from thirty four league matches. They lost all of their last eight league fixtures and on eight occasions they conceded thirty points or more in addition to the twelve occasions on which they failed to score more than five points. The top try scorer was 'Ziggy' Piwinski with seven tries. These statistics stand in sharp contrast to those of the previous season, so what is the explanation? There is no doubt that the team was affected by the departures of Martyn and Gittins in addition to the speculation and denials which preceded the transfer of these two key players. There was also more chopping and changing with regard to team selection, a feature which militated against the creation of a cohesive team. Both of these factors contributed to underperformance on a grand scale.

Batley recovered somewhat during 1972-1973, winning fifteen of their thirty four league fixtures. Indeed, they made a very good start to the season with ten victories from their first fourteen matches, one of which was the defeat of Hunslet by twenty six points to three in a John Player cup-tie. The team also managed to score four tries on eleven occasions and Jim Naylor was selected to play for the county.

Disappointingly, Batley faltered at the end of the season, winning only two of their last ten league matches. More promisingly, there was a reasonable distribution of tries amongst the backs: Phil Holmes (13); Keith Toohey (13); Geoff Marsh (13) and Steve Lingard, who had been recruited during the previous season, (11). There was hope that a new platform had been established as the basis for further improvement, particularly as the squad had been strengthened by the acquisition of Robin Dewhurst in November 1972.

Sadly, the desired improvement did not take place. From the start of the 1973-1974 season to the end of the 1978-1979 season Batley won only thirty nine of their one hundred and fifty six league matches, precisely twenty five percent. In fact the 1973-1974 season, at the start of which Batley had recruited Keith Cotton, Tony Dean, Alan Hepworth and Graham Stocks, was by some margin the most successful season of this fairly dismal run. During this season Batley recorded twelve victories from twenty six league games, managing to score four or more tries on six occasions. But for a sequence of poor results, running from the end of December 1973 to the middle of February 1974, during which Batley lost seven of their eight league fixtures, this may have been a significantly more successful season. Phil Holmes was the top try scorer with twelve tries, followed by Geoff Marsh, Alan Watts and Dave Brooke each of whom scored four tries. The last, appearing in every game played during the season, also kicked sixty goals. One of the highlights of the season, in addition to the defeat of Hull KR by twenty three points to eight in the first round of the Yorkshire Cup, was the way in which Batley overturned a sixteen point deficit carried into the second leg of their second division play-off game against Workington. When Batley conceded two early penalties, thus trailing by twenty points on aggregate, it seemed that there was no way back for the 'Gallant Youths'. In a stirring performance, through tries by John Fox, Phil Holmes, Steve Grinhaff and Keith Cotton and five goals by Brooke and one by Blakeway, Batley won on aggregate by thirty three points to twenty nine. The euphoria was short-lived as Batley were defeated by Bradford Northern in the next round.

For the remainder of the decade, with the exception of the final season, Batley struggled to win even a quarter of the league games played per season. Sometimes, as in the 1974-1975 season when they did not win a match until the 26th October 1974, the team made a very poor start to the new season, thereby increasing the pressure on the players. Throughout the whole of the 1974-1975 season, in which they played twenty six league games, Batley only had five victories and one draw. More significantly, during this season, there were ten matches played in which Batley failed to score a try and only one game in which the team scored four tries. Unsurprisingly, the leading try scorer for this season, Phil Holmes, scored only nine tries.

An attempt was made to strengthen the team for the following season with the acquisition of Dave Rippon and John Harrison, both of whom made their debuts at the end of the 1974-1975 season, and Peter Jameson, whose first appearance for Batley was at the start of the new campaign in August 1975. There was a glimmer of hope that this would be a significantly more successful season when, during the last two weeks of September and the first week of October 1975, Batley achieved three consecutive victories, one of which was in a John Player cup-tie. Alas, this hope was forlorn as the team registered only four more victories before the end of the season, leaving Batley with a total of six wins from twenty six league games. In fact, Batley did not win a single match from their last nine league fixtures, conceding one hundred and fifty eight points whilst scoring only forty eight. This time, the new recruit, John Harrison, was the leading try scorer with eight tries. It was also at the end of this season that Steve Presley, who eventually made more than two hundred appearances for Batley, made his debut, whilst Ernie Hepworth celebrated his tenth season at Batley.

Disappointment after Early Promise

The statistics for this season reveal the nature of Batley's problem during this period. The team found it difficult to score tries. During the 1975-1976 season, Batley scored fifteen points or more on only four occasions and failed to score more than five points on eleven occasions.

There was a slight improvement in the team's performance during the 1976-1977 season, a season in which Alan Watts, who had made his debut in October 1969, played his 200th game for Batley. The team secured seven wins and one draw from twenty six league games, suffering seven consecutive defeats during the winter period from mid-November 1976 to early January 1977. On a more positive note, Batley failed to score any points on only one occasion, unfortunately in the New Year's match against Dewsbury. More worryingly, the statistics indicate that the team had significant defensive frailties since Batley played thirteen matches in which the team conceded twenty or more points.

Seasons, 1977-1978 and 1978-1979, were memorable for the wrong reasons. During the former, Batley only secured five wins and one draw from twenty six league fixtures in addition to which the board of directors was involved in an acrimonious dispute with the Supporters' Club, more about which will be explored later. With only one victory from their first seven league games, Batley made a very poor start to this season and finished it as disappointingly with only two wins from their last ten league fixtures. Once again Batley played thirteen matches in which they conceded twenty or more points, whilst there was only one game in which they scored twenty or more points. The recruitment of Dave Stockwell, Brendan Finn, Jim Waltham and John Simpson at the start of the season did not have the desired effect, whilst this must have been a particularly arduous season for Dave Rippon, who played in every single match.

The 1978-1979 season, in which Batley registered only four wins and one draw from twenty six league matches, was the second worst of the decade with regard to results. Henry Oulton, who eventually played more than one hundred and fifty games and kicked more than four hundred goals for Batley, and Keith Riggs both made their debuts during this season, but to little avail. Winning only one of their first sixteen league matches, Batley made their worst ever start to a season. They were consistent in so far as they once more played thirteen games in which they conceded twenty or more points, in addition to which the 'Gallant Youths ' failed to score a try in almost one third of the league and cup games played during the season. The new recruit, Henry Oulton, topped the list of try scorers with five tries. Perhaps the most uplifting news of this season was the report in the *Batley News*, 19th October 1978 about Ike Fowler's visit to Swansea to watch the Rugby League International between Wales and Australia. Apparently, David Oxley, the Rugby League Secretary, had arranged a complimentary seat in the stand for Ike, who was invited to meet the Welsh team in the dressing room.

For the final season of the decade, 1979-1980, during which John Fox had his testimonial after ten years at the club, Batley had new directors, a new coaching staff and some new players. Tommy Smales, assisted by Trevor Lowe, took over as coach and the playing squad was strengthened with the addition of Trevor Briggs, Steve Brunyee and John Vodden. In the end, ten victories and two draws from twenty six league fixtures could hardly be described as a bumper season, but by comparison with the previous two seasons it was a relatively successful one for Batley. At least the number of wins was more than the combined total of victories from those two seasons. There is no doubt that during the 1970s Batley fans had to be grateful for small mercies.

Disappointment after Early Promise

The Supporters' Club

The minute book in which meetings of the Supporters' Club during the period November 1972 to May 1982 were recorded reveals some telling details about the activities and concerns of its members. As might be expected in connection with a rugby league club that was often strapped for cash, a substantial amount of the members' time and energy was devoted to discussing, planning and taking part in activities designed to raise money for Batley RLFC. Numerous raffles and jumble sales were organised during this period, with the latter sometimes involving the hire of a stall at Batley Market. Indeed, the frequency with which jumble sales were held 1972-1978 suggests that members of the Supporters' Club were global leaders with regard to recycling! Interestingly, from early 1978 onwards there is no record of any jumble sales. Fund raising activities in general seem to have been suspended from January 1978 to April 1979, during which time the Supporter's Club was in dispute with the Board of Directors of Batley RLFC, but once this dispute had been resolved it was business as usual, except for jumble sales. Given the emergence and growth of car boot sales in the 1970s, it is possible that it was neither feasible nor economic to continue with jumble sales. One of the most successful money making activities, organised in 1975, was the Donkey Derby, which raised £200.

Allied to, though separate from direct fund raising events, was the provision of fast food at home games. This, of course, helped to raise money for the Supporters' Club, which made at least one donation annually to Batley RLFC, but involved some risk in so far as potential sales had to be estimated before the food was ordered from the suppliers. In the event of a last minute postponement, the Supporters'

Club could be left with a substantial amount of unsold food on its hands. At almost every meeting which took place during the playing season there is reference to the number of pies and sausage rolls to be ordered for the next home game. If the visiting team was Doncaster, it was likely to be five dozen pies, whereas for a cup tie against Wigan the order could be for twenty dozen pies. In the event of a home game being called off at short notice, as in December 1973, members of the Supporters' Club committee came to the rescue, purchasing the surplus pies and sausage rolls at 4p and 2p per item respectively. Care was also taken with regard to the quality of the produce, as when the decision was taken that no pies should be ordered for the Boxing Day game in 1973 because, as a result of the holiday, they would not be fresh. Nor should it be said that the Supporters' Club could not embrace change. In October 1975 the decision was made to sell cartons of soup at home games! The minutes also tell us something about the inflationary pressures which existed during this ten year period. Between March 1973 and September 1977 the price of a pie more than doubled as it rose from 7p to 15p.

On an annual basis, the Supporters' Club made arrangements for a Players' Awards Night, assisted with the organisation of reunions for ex-players, liaised with the Yorkshire Federation of Rugby League Supporters' Clubs, as well as organising quiz nights and rugby league forums to which individuals such as Peter Fox, David Oxley, David Howes and Albert Fearnley were invited. In doing so, members of the Supporters' Club committee had to make arrangements with venues such as the Taverners and the Lakeside Lodge, Wilton Park. Such was the commitment to these activities that even at the height of its dispute with the Batley RLFC Board of Directors in February 1978, the

Disappointment after Early Promise

Supporters' Club went ahead with arrangements for a players' reunion at the Lakeside Lodge.

It is clear from the minutes of their meetings that a perennial concern for the Supporters' Club was the maintenance of the property it owned, be it the renewal or installation of electrical wiring, the repair of burst pipes and leaking roofs, the need for the internal and external painting of tea/refreshment huts or repairs incurred as a result of break-ins. All of these maintenance needs put pressure on the Supporters' Club's limited funds, with the result that non-essential repairs had to be delayed until money was available. Nonetheless, of enormous help in these circumstances were the materials and labour provided free of charge by members of the Supporters' Club.

Without doubt, one of the most valuable services provided by the Supporters' Club, particularly during a period in which car ownership was limited, was the chartering of coaches for away games. Ultimately, by the early 1980s, excursions to games in Cumbria were no longer economic, but 1972-1982 the Supporters' Club arranged a coach service, at a very reasonable cost, to most away games. Occasionally the Minutes record the committee's frustration with those who, having booked a seat on the coach, failed to turn up, thereby delaying the departure of the coach and causing inconvenience to everybody on the coach. In one instance, however, the boot was on the other foot. In October 1975 it was agreed that the chairman of the Supporters' Club Committee should offer an apology to a supporter who had arrived at the pickup point in Birstall three minutes late only to find that the coach had departed.

An issue which was a regular concern for the Supporters' Club in 1972-1982 was the perceived lack of publicity for Batley RLFC in the local press. In April 1973 the minutes record the members' disappointment at the absence of the local press, in spite of an invitation to attend, from the Players' Awards ceremony, whilst in May 1976 a letter was sent to the editor of the *Batley News* asking why no photos of it had appeared in the newspaper. Worse was to come, for by February 1980 the perception was that, horror of horrors, Dewsbury RLFC was being given more publicity in the *Batley News* than Batley RLFC and a letter from the Supporters' Club requesting an explanation for this disparity was promptly despatched to the *Batley News*. The consensus within the Supporters' Club was that the problem lay with the editor. Perhaps he was a closet Dewsbury fan!

In October 1973 the minutes record a very interesting item relating to the influence of sponsors. John Winner, who had attended a meeting of the Yorkshire Federation of Supporters' Clubs, reported to a Batley Supporters' Club meeting that officials from the Yorkshire County Rugby League had explained to the Federation that the final of the Yorkshire County Cup would be played at Headingley, irrespective of the teams contesting the final, on the insistence of Esso, the competition's sponsors; an early example of the compromises that come with sponsorship.

On three occasions the minutes make reference to Supporters' Club members' concerns about the unacceptable behaviour of both home and visiting fans, one case referring to the cutting down of a flag at Mount Pleasant by Hull FC fans. However, given the increasing level of violence at even minor football clubs during the 1970s, this was small beer.

In addition to the wide range of activities already outlined, the Supporters' Club also had to manage relations with the cricket club, the bowling club and, when Hunslet RLFC were playing their home games at Mount Pleasant, with Hunslet Supporters' Club, all of whom wished to make use of facilities that belonged to Batley RLSC. For the most part relations were amicable. Hunslet Supporters' Club paid for the use of both the souvenir shop and the tea hut. However, it seems that the reluctance of the Taverners' Bowling Club to pay for the use of a hut behind the Taverners' led to the demolition of the hut.

By far the most dramatic event of the period 1972-1982 was the dispute between the Supporters' Club and the Board of Directors of Batley RLFC which led to the Board dissolving the Supporters' Club in January 1978. The dispute, which had been brewing for some time, was rooted in the Supporters' Club's dissatisfaction with the way in which the Board of Directors was running Batley RLFC and particularly with regard to its perceived lack of interest in the Supporters' Club. The claim was that the Board liked to receive its annual cheques from the Supporters' Club but was deaf to any criticism. The dispute escalated to the point where the Supporters' Club took legal advice about a "break-in" at the small tea hut (the property of the Supporters' Club) by members of the Board of Directors and refused to organise any money-making activities. The dispute was even reported in the national press in addition to coverage in local newspapers. Below are a series of extracts which convey a flavour of the conflict:

Batley News, 5th January 1978

Ewart Earnshaw said "we have looked to them for support but they have developed into an angry group which is not helping football at Mount Pleasant. We've all got complaints and what would happen if the directors went on strike? A number of directors paid Albert Fearnley's salary out of their own pockets and, having done that, bent over backwards to retain him. It wasn't our fault that he left. We've asked the Supporters' Club to send a delegation to us and they have refused. There is an open invitation to meet us at any board meeting"

Mr Harry Myers, chairman of the Supporters' Club, wanted the full committee of six to attend a meeting with the directors. He said "during our last meeting at the Taverners' Club, Mr. Driver, the club chairman, was seen at an adjacent bar and was cordially invited to meet us. He declined."

With regard to the activities from which the Supporters' Club had withdrawn Mr Earnshaw claimed that the board were organising them, as they had in the past. He said " We let the Supporters' Club do those jobs so that they could have some money, while the tea making is something that can be dealt with if they are going to continue with the strike. There are a number of people anxious to serve on a development committee. A number of clubs have such committees already. They are not associated with supporters' clubs and cannot co-exist with them. They are more forward looking."

Mr Myers said "As far as I am concerned there were no teas or refreshments sold at Mount Pleasant last week, while the people who were working in the car park were the club secretary and an ex-director."

Letter from Bill Winner, *Batley News*, 12th January 1978

Having been a supporter of Batley Rugby League Club for 30 years, 17 of those years as a member of the Supporters' Club Committee, I feel I must reply to certain statements which have recently appeared in the press.

Mr. Earnshaw asks what would happen if the directors went on strike. I put it to Mr. Earnshaw – how long is it since he had a full complement of directors at a meeting or a match? That is to say, the nine who have their names in the Batley programme.

No, Mr. Earnshaw, the dispute goes much further back than Albert Fearnley, though I admit that brought things to a head.

Disappointment after Early Promise

Certain things have hurt the committee over the years, such as the non-attendance of directors at the Supporters' Club annual meetings, only one director at the 50th anniversary celebrations, and the movement of the committee room and tea room to a point well away from the ground where it has become a white elephant.

The Supporters' Club committee is not strong, having lost six members since October 1977, leaving us with just seven.

Thanks must go to the directors for letting us have some money from the car park and programme sales, but we were led to believe by one director that this was helping you also, as takings on both these had gone up, but there again, the same director informed us that the home games for 1977/78 would be sponsored and a commercial director would be employed.

How the new development committee will work I don't know. I wish it luck, but I seem to remember two gentlemen making quite a bit of money for the club – and not many years ago at that – only for their aspirations to be dashed..

Turning to Mr. Driver, I would say that the Supporters' Club will not be left out in the cold. We shall be like the others who have left Mount Pleasant, at home in the warmth.

In closing, I would like to say that from season 1959-60 to season 1976-77 the Supporters' Club Committee handed over £1,900 and spent £1,625 on ground repairs and the purchase of committee and tea huts. Not much, you may say, in 18 years, but considering the state of the club during most of those years, a commendable effort.

To the Batley public I say thank you for your support of the Supporters' Club in the past years.

Daily Express, 13th January 1978

In January 1978 Batley's board of directors, headed by Chairman Leslie Driver and President Ewart Earnshaw, dissolved the 51 year old Batley Supporters' Club. This rather drastic action was

taken in the wake of a "strike" by the members of the Supporters'
Club with regard to money making activities. The Supporters'
Club had resorted to this action as a result of dissatisfaction with
the board of directors which had come to a head following the
departure of Batley's coach Albert Fearnley in October.
Supporters' Club members withdrew from supervising car parks,
operating refreshment counters and selling programmes because
the directors had refused to meet them to discuss their grievances.
Les Driver said "the actions of the group were those of 'angry
men' who wanted to cause trouble because they were disappointed
that Albert Fearnley had left as coach earlier in the season"

Yorkshire Evening Post, 31st January 1978
The board of directors supported the formation of a Development
Committee and Leslie Driver said "there would not be room for
both organisations." Driver said that he had been approached by
about 12 supporters who were not interested in joining the
Supporters' Club and wanted to form a Development Committee.
"I understand there are plenty more also interested who do not agree
with the action of the Supporters' Club"

Nonetheless, although the Supporters' Club held no meetings
between 2nd October 1978 and 23rd April 1979, relations
were repaired with a new Board of Directors in July 1979.

In fact the dispute appears to have revitalised the
Supporters' Club. From July 1979 there was a substantial
increase in numbers attending its meetings. One of the
principal functions of the Supporters' Club was to raise
money, some of which could then be handed over to Batley
RLFC. By 10th May 1982 the Batley RLSC account had a
healthy balance of £1525.

Afterword

THE CENTENARY YEAR AND BEYOND

The 1980-1981 season was Batley RLFC's centenary season, which was marked by the production of a range of merchandise including ties, sweaters and crockery, in addition to the organisation of re-unions for ex-players and a Centenary Dinner Dance at the Town Hall.

The season itself was a rather disappointing one for the club as Batley won only eleven of their twenty eight league matches. That having been said, they did finish the season on a more positive note, winning seven of their last nine fixtures. The damage had been done in the first part of the season during which Batley won only three of their first thirteen league matches. A better start to the season might well have resulted in a league position which was more fitting for a proud club celebrating its centenary.

The designated centenary game was the home fixture against Fulham in April 1981, a match that Batley won by ten points to eight courtesy of a try by Briggs and Henry Oulton's three goals and a drop goal. At half time, many former Batley players from different eras, having gathered on the pitch, received generous applause from the crowd of approximately four thousand spectators. The Centenary Dinner Dance, held at the end of the season, sadly had one very noticeable absentee, George Harwood, a director who had played a key role in organising events for the centenary season, but who had died the day before the Centenary Dinner Dance.

The 1980s brought debuts for players such as John Jones, August 1980, Paul Storey and Mick Wilson, September 1981, Carl Gibson, April 1982, John Stainburn, September 1983, Neil Illingworth, October 1984, John Carroll, December 1984, Andy Williams, September 1985, Simon Wilson, February 1986, Paul Gearey and Steve Parrish, December 1987, Mark Bownass, April 1988 and Neil Kellett, February 1989. This was also the decade in which, for two consecutive seasons (1980-1982), Steve Pressley played in every single game. However, it was only the mid-1980s that could be described as a successful period for the team during this decade. In the 1984-1985 season, Batley won seventeen of their twenty eight league games as Carl Gibson repeated his achievement from the previous season in equalling George Gabriel's post-war record of twenty six tries. The following season, during which Gibson scored thirteen tries in eighteen appearances, Batley recorded seventeen victories and three draws from thirty four league games. Clearly, this fast, powerful and stylish centre three-quarter, who was selected to play for Great Britain in March 1985, was the key component in Batley's improved performance. Inevitably, as in the past, Batley could not hold on to a player of this quality and in 1986 he was transferred to Leeds.

Apart from the middle seasons of the decade, Batley once more struggled in the 1980s, this in spite of the commendable efforts of Gerald Cox, the coach of the Batley Boys Under-19 team, to feed young players through to the senior squad. A low point during the 1980s was the 1982-1983 season in which Batley registered only six victories and one draw from thirty three league matches. In spite of the efforts of Carl Gibson, who scored fifteen tries in his first full season for the club, Batley could only win one of their last twenty one league matches. As in the recent past, Batley frequently struggled to win more than a quarter of the matches played. Thus by the end of the 1980s the time was ripe for a change.

It came in the form of Stephen Ball, who took over as chairman of Batley RLFC in 1989. He brought a new dynamic energy to the club, arranging a sponsorship deal with Fox's Biscuits, setting up a new company, Batley Rugby Taverners Club, which took over The Taverners and initiating the 'Buy a Brick' scheme to help fund the construction of a new stand. Steve was at Batley until 1995 and in 1994 the team came within one victory of promotion to Division 1 for the first time in the club's history. Unfortunately, Batley, hampered by Jeff Grayshon's dismissal, lost the crunch game against Doncaster by ten points to five at Mount Pleasant on 24th April 1994. One year later, Batley were in contention once again, only this time promotion to Division 1, along with Keighley, seemed assured. Dave Hadfield, writing in *The Independent*, 5th April 1995 under the heading 'Batley's Firm Foundation, wrote:

Batley are preparing for the First Division by ploughing their resources into bricks and mortar rather than flesh and blood. The club, bottom of the League, bankrupt and derelict when the present board took over six years ago, yesterday unveiled a 2,250 capacity £500,000 stand, in readiness for what is now almost certain promotion to the First Division for the first time in their hundred year history.

Hadfield, highlighting the fact that the funds from the new stand had primarily come from the City Challenge Scheme, then explained how Stephen Ball preferred to prepare Batley for entry into the First Division by spending money on facilities rather than players, assets whose value could be quickly dissipated in the event of a serious injury. The article quoted Ball saying: "We are the most financially competent club in the game. We have no debts and our extra income in the First Division will be just that – extra income."

In the event the dreams of the Batley fans were shattered. Batley did, along with Keighley, qualify for promotion to the First Division, but the timing could not have been worse as it coincided with the decision to set up the Super League, from which Batley and Keighley were excluded. It goes without saying that this decision caused a great deal of anger and resentment amongst Batley, and no doubt Keighley, fans, who felt that the club had been cheated out of a promotion that it had legitimately earned. Debates about the benefits of the Super League for both the game as a whole and for teams such as Batley continue unto this day, but the complexities involved in these debates are a matter for discussion elsewhere. Suffice to say that, though Batley was given £500,000 compensation in lieu of promotion, the sense of grievance experienced by Batley fans in 1995 was very real.

Following the departure of Stephen Ball in 1995 there was a period of turmoil at the club stemming largely from a struggle within the board of directors, a struggle which, according to the present chairman, Kevin Nicholas, brought Batley RLFC to the brink of liquidation. In short, Kevin Nicholas's view is that his predecessor as chairman, Trevor Hobson, had allowed Batley to take on too much debt. As creditor for some of that debt, Trevor Hobson, once he was ousted as chairman, exerted pressure on the club for payment of what he was owed. It was this in combination with demands from other creditors, mainly small businesses which needed the money, which almost resulted in disaster for Batley RLFC. In the end the finances were stabilised and the club survived.

In 1998, Batley, known as Batley Bulldogs since the introduction of summer rugby, won the Trans Pennine Cup, beating Oldham at Mount Pleasant, their first trophy since 1924. However, few fans will forget Batley's dramatic victory by twenty five points to twenty four against Widnes in the final of the Northern Rail Cup at Blackpool in 2010. Having led by twelve points to nil, Batley trailed Widnes by twenty four points to fifteen with just thirteen minutes of the match left, thirteen minutes in which two tries by Alex Brown, along with a Gareth Moore conversion, secured a stunning victory for Batley. The winning try was described in the *Yorkshire Evening Post*, 19th July 2010, as follows:

It looked as though the Vikings would hold on, but with two minutes left Moore hoisted a perfect kick to the corner on the last tackle. Brown leaped above Shaun Ainscough to make a wonderful catch, managing to hold on and plant the ball down over the line.

Batley's victory in the Northern Rail Cup, when the coach was Karl Harrison, was, perhaps, equalled by their third place finish in the Championship in 2016 under the guidance of the coach, John Kear, a feat which earned them a place in the Super 8 Qualifiers.

It is perhaps fitting for a club with such a rich history that, as this book goes to press, Batley Bulldogs employs two renowned former players in key roles: chief executive Paul Harrison, who holds the record at Batley for most tries scored by a forward, and newly appointed coach, Craig Lingard, Batley's all-time leading try scorer.